WEAVING WITH RIBBON

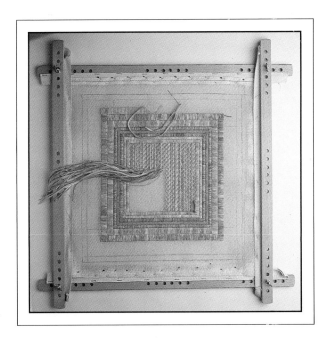

WEAVING WITH RIBBON

Valerie Campbell-Harding

DAVID & CHARLES

A David & Charles craft book

Acknowledgements

The author thanks those students who allowed their
samples to be photographed for this book. Special
thanks also to Jane Lemon for help and advice, and for
making the file cover and burse (pages 45, 46) and to
Jenny Blackburn for making the fishing net jacket on
page 59.

Acknowledgements and thanks also to the following
companies for providing materials for this book:
Beresford and Panda for ribbons
C.M. Offray & Son Ltd for ribbons
Madeira Threads Ltd for embroidery threads
The Vilene Organisation, Halifax, England (Pellon,
USA) for iron-on interfacings.
Simplicity Style patterns for baby gown reference (page
101).

Note: Unless otherwise indicated, samples and designs
have been worked by the author.

British Library Cataloguing in Publication Data

Weaving with ribbon
1   Ribbons   2   Handicraft
I. Title
Campbell-Harding, Valerie
746.2'7 TT880
ISBN 0-7153-8924-6

Special photography by Di Lewis
Diagram artwork by Southern Flair Ltd, Eastbourne,
East Sussex
Phototypeset by Central Southern Typesetters
Eastbourne, East Sussex
Printed in Hong Kong by Regent Publishing Services
Ltd for David & Charles Publishers plc
Brunel House   Newton Abbot   Devon

Distributed in the United States of America
by Sterling Publishing Co, Inc, 2 Park Avenue,
New York, NY 10016

Contents

Weaving with ribbon

Weaving ribbons through other ribbons is an ancient craft and has its origins in weaving itself. In recent years, with the development of polyester piece-dyed and washable ribbons, ribbon weaving has revived as a modern crafts technique and the resulting fabric can be used to make all kinds of furnishings, accessories and clothing.

Ribbon weaving patterns can be simple or complex, and can be varied by mixing ribbons of different widths, colours and textures. Because they are beautiful and luxurious, things made with ribbons are always something special and treasured.

Once having tried weaving ribbons through ribbons, there is then the challenge of developing the craft, to widen the perimeters of accepted techniques and experimenting with new and different bases for weaving ribbons. For instance, ribbons can be woven through fabrics such as net or canvas, these fabrics dyed or printed to alter their colour or machine-stitched to add texture and contrast with the ribbons. Fabric can also be constructed for weaving with knitting and crochet stitches. Ribbons can be woven through threads and embroidery stitches, or through unusual substances, such as sequin waste. The resulting effects will encourage further experimentation and there may be no limits to the combinations of ribbons and base materials.

About this book
In this book, you'll find ideas for different kinds of weaves and new combinations of techniques. Each chapter then provides projects for you to try the ideas for yourself. Although detailed instructions are given, these can be adapted and altered as you wish to make the article different and more individual. Alternative colour schemes are also given.

Variations and experiments have been suggested in each chapter, and the projects can be adapted to include any one of them. Finally, there is a section on further experiments and more complex work.

There are so many possibilities using ribbon weaving that this book can only suggest a few of them, but when you have tried some of the weaves and made one or two items, your own ideas will take over and lead you along a totally new path to something even more exciting.

Types of ribbon
Modern ribbons come in a vast range of colours and patterns. They are usually made of nylon or polyester, and in widths from 1.5mm (1/16 in) wide to 52mm (2¼ in) wide, although not all widths are available in every type of ribbon.

Satin Both single-faced and double-faced satin ribbons are available. Single-faced satin is more suitable for weaving as the back does not usually show and the dull 'wrong' side can sometimes provide an additional texture. This ribbon has a beautiful lustre and comes in plain colours, stripes and in printed patterns. ▶

Woven and embroidered ribbons: from the top, a late nineteenth-century woven ribbon, a modern woven ribbon, a nineteenth-century ribbon with the flowers stuffed from the back, two modern woven ribbons, patterned and plain ribbons decorated with machine-embroidery, an Indian ribbon woven with gold thread

Taffeta This is softer than satin ribbon, and can be made of nylon or polyester. It comes in plain colours, checks, tartans, moiré and in printed patterns.

Velvet This ribbon, available in nylon polyester or cotton, has a pile texture which contrasts superbly with smooth-surfaced ribbons. Colours are rich and jewel-like, and ribbons are sometimes edged with gold or silver thread.

Grosgrain This ribbon is stiffer than satin and has ribbed texture. It is very good for articles which need 'body'. There is a good variety of plain colours and stripes and printed spots are also available.

Woven and Jaquard patterns Most of these are floral designs but geometric patterns are also manufactured. Some include metallic threads in the pattern.

Lurex These ribbons add glitter and a luxury look to items and come in plain weaves in gold, silver and copper, some edged with coloured threads.

Fancy edges Some ribbons are decorated on the edges with Lurex threads, picots, feather knots, scalloped or crochet edges. These decorative edges show well when woven with plain ribbons.

Knitting ribbon This is a much softer ribbon to use, and comes in a 6mm (¼ in) width only. There is a good range of colours.

Cut-edged and flower ribbons These ribbons are cut, like slices, from a roll of stiffened acetate fabric and will fray if they are washed. They can, however, be used for experiments or for short-lived articles such as Christmas decorations.

Rayon knitting ribbon This is also a tubular yarn, and has a very shiny finish. Sometimes a metallic thread is included. The shine of these ribbons provides contrast when used with matt ribbons.

Metallic knitting ribbons These are also tubular in structure and are usually imported. They are very rich and subtle in colour and can be threaded with wool or cotton to add bulk.

Cotton knitting ribbon This is a tubular yarn with a matt finish. It is very soft and can be threaded with thick wool to make it fat and rounded (like rouleau). Different manufacturers produce different widths. The colour range is not extensive, but the ribbon can easily be dyed.

Flat knitting tapes These are made of rayon or nylon, sometimes with an open weave that looks like net.

Strips of fabric, lengths of raffia, leather thongs or sewing tape can also be used in conjunction with ribbons.

If you want something different for a particular project it is worth searching for imported or antique ribbons. Indian ribbons for instance, often have a woven pattern with metallic threads and these can sometimes be found in shops that specialise in Indian textiles. Japanese ribbons are more difficult to obtain but are lustrous and well-worth searching for. Antique ribbons are often found in shops that sell period clothes, as they are used to refurbish garments. These old ribbons are usually much softer than modern ones, and sometimes the colour is shaded from one edge to the other. Some have wonderful woven and embossed patterns, and these ribbons can be combined with new ribbons for a different look.

Colour schemes

Colour is exciting and is the most important part of your work, but many people find it the most difficult part: here are some suggestions of ways to choose colour schemes.

Colour in nature A close look at a flower, a feather, a shell, a fruit or vegetable, will show some surprising combinations of colours. For instance, a red-skinned apple might have touches of very bright green, and a little yellow. Or, what at first sight appears to be plain grey stone wall might, on closer examination, have some blue patches in the stone, with patches of bright orange-yellow lichen growing on it. A creamy-white rose will be seen to have touches of blue-pink deep inside in the shadows, with orange stamens. Note down the approximate proportions of the various colours and, when planning a colour scheme, refer to them, as it is never successful to have equal quantities of different colours in a design. Take your notes, (and the inspiration also, if possible) when you go to buy the ribbons and match the colours as closely as you can. If three-quarters of the rose-inspired colour scheme is creamy-white, then this colour could be in either one length of very wide ribbon, or in several lengths of very narrow ribbons.

Working in one colour

Choose a single colour, such as blue. Find as many variations of blue as you can, a green-blue, a mauve-blue and a dull grey-blue and combine the colours. Use different textures of ribbons of one range of colour together as this affects the colour scheme and produces very exciting effects.

Working in colour families

Choose colours that are near to each other in the spectrum, such as reds, oranges and yellow, or blues, mauves and pinks. Look in the garden for ideas for similar combinations of close-related colours, and you will be surprised at how many different variations there are.

Working with contrasting colours

Two strongly contrasting colours such as red and green or blue and orange, can look too vibrant; the trick is to have a large quantity of one colour, a very small amount of the other, and to use shade variations of both colours. For instance, varying greens – some bright, some dull, some dark, some pale, used with a small amount of red, will make a beautiful and harmonious concept. Here again, inspiration will be found in nature. A holly tree with berries, you will observe, is mainly made up of different shades of green, with touches of bright red.

Working with neutrals

It is often thought that neutral colours are safe, when in fact they can be extremely dull if used alone. However, if cream, mushroom and bright pink are combined, or white, grey and yellow, or beige and apricot with touches of orange are put together, then the neutrals become an exciting contrast to the colours. Again, the trick is to vary the proportions and have small amounts of the brighter colours.

Equipment required in ribbon weaving

You will probably have most of the tools and equipment that you need to weave with ribbons, but the following items will be particularly useful:

- Sharp scissors, about 12.5cm (5 in) long.
- Glass-headed pins, which are easier to see and use than steel pins.
- A water soluble pen. These were designed to be used on man-made fabrics only, so they are ideal for marking a pattern on a woven ribbon.
- A cork bath mat, for pinning work to. (A piece of insulating board would do as an alternative, or a large piece of expanding polystyrene packing.)
- A large-sized needle for weaving very narrow ribbons.
- A ball-pointed bodkin for weaving ribbons through fabric.
- Pelmet-weight non-woven interfacing for stiffening bags and cases.
- Iron-on interfacing for backing ribbon weaving.

CHAPTER ONE

Decorating ribbons

Ribbons come in many different colours but even so you may sometimes find that the one subtle shade you want to complete a colour scheme is not available. It may then be necessary to dye white ribbon to get the colour you want. Cotton and nylon rbbons can be coloured with hot-water dyes.

Alternatively, although ribbons are beautiful in themselves, you might want to paint or print on them. The space-dyeing, sponge-painting, block-printing, tritik and marbling techniques in this chapter will give an individual look to your work.

Ribbons can also be decorated with stitching and this changes not only the colour but can add glitter, as well as giving the ribbon a beautiful handle.

Two or three of the decorating methods described here might be combined in one piece of work, together with plain ribbons, to add a little 'spice' to the design.

Dyeing in plain colours

To dye cotton or nylon ribbon, use a hot-water dye, usually sold in small tin containers. Tip the dye powder into a bowl and mix to a paste with a little cold water. For about 150g (5 oz) of ribbon, put 2 litres (4 pints) of water into a large, old saucepan, add the dye and 1 × 15ml spoon (1 tablespoon) of salt. Stir to mix. Bring slowly to the boil.

Meanwhile, soak the ribbons in cold water. When the dye water is almost boiling, add the drained ribbons to the saucepan. Boil for 15 to 30 minutes, stirring frequently with a wooden stick to avoid blotches of colour on the ribbon. A longer boiling produces a deeper colour. Lift out the ribbons, rinse them in several changes of water and hang to dry them naturally.

If the finished colour is not exactly the tone needed, the ribbons can be dyed again in a fresh dye-bath.

Space-dyed ribbons

Space-dyeing is the term used for random dyeing where ribbons are given a multi-coloured effect along their length. With just a red, a yellow and a blue dye, almost every colour you want can be obtained. This method uses cold-water dye and is only suitable for cotton, silk or rayon ribbons.

Method

Arrange white or cream ribbon round the bottom of a shallow container – an old baking dish will do. Mix ¼ × 5ml spoon (¼ teaspoon) of red dye powder to a paste in a jar with a little cold water and add 1 × 5ml spoon (1 teaspoon) of salt. Do the same with the yellow dye in another jar, and mix the blue dye in a third. Add sufficient hot water to each jar to dissolve the dye powder, but do not fill the jar more than half full. Spoon the yellow dye onto the ribbons at intervals until it has all been used (Fig 1, page 12). Do the same with the red dye and finally spoon on the blue dye. Leave for 5 minutes to allow the dye to soak into the fabric.

Right: This weaving example was achieved with hand-made paper made with ribbon in it. Slits were cut in the paper and narrow ribbons woven through. The paper was then cut into strips and woven with wider machine-stitched ribbons

Meanwhile, mix 2 × 15ml spoons (2 table-spoons) of washing soda with ½ litre (1 pint) of hot water and stir until dissolved. Pour the mixture over the ribbons. Leave for 30 minutes to fix the dye.

Pour away the fixing solution and remaining dye and rinse the ribbons thoroughly in several changes of cold water until the water is clear and no more colour comes out. Mix a little detergent with enough boiling water to cover the ribbons in a bowl, and leave for 15 minutes. Rinse again and hang the ribbons to dry.

The ribbons may need smoothing with a moderately hot iron.

Painting on ribbons

Fabric paints, unlike dyes, can be used on ribbons made of any natural or man-made fibre. These paints can be sponged onto the ribbon, printed or painted on with a brush. The colour is fixed by ironing for one minute at a temperature suitable for the type of ribbon. It is important to use colours all of one make as different brands will not necessarily mix with each other.

Sponge-painted ribbons

A random coloured effect similar to space-dyeing can be obtained by sponge-painting.

Method

Lay the ribbons flat on newspaper. Mix 1 × 5ml spoon (1 teaspoon) of fabric paint with twice as much water, and dab it onto the ribbons with a small sponge. Leave plenty of white areas between the dabs of colour. Mix a second colour and dab it on between the areas of the first colour. Mix a third colour if you wish and dab it on. The colours can sometimes be allowed to overlap and will run together while they are wet to make other colours.

Leave the ribbons to dry. It will be seen that the colours become paler when dry. Iron the ribbons for 1 minute, following the manufacturer's instructions, to set the colour.

Block-printed ribbons

Block-printing is a method of making repeat patterns on textiles. The pattern need not be regular, and used on ribbon, a fluidity of design is possible which is not always achieved with woven-patterned ribbons.

Blocks for printing can be made of carved wood, from a piece of lino or can be half a potato. For abstract designs, try the effect of string glued to a piece of thick card. Objects such as straws, corks, bottle tops etc will also print interesting shapes which can be used to build up a design.

Method

Spread the ribbon flat on a clean work surface. Use fabric paint straight from the pot, and, with a paint brush, apply a very little onto the printing block. If too much colour is used, it may run on the ribbon and spoil the print. Press the block firmly onto the ribbon then lift off cleanly. Brush a little more paint

Fig 1 Space-dyeing: spoon the dye colour onto the ribbon at intervals

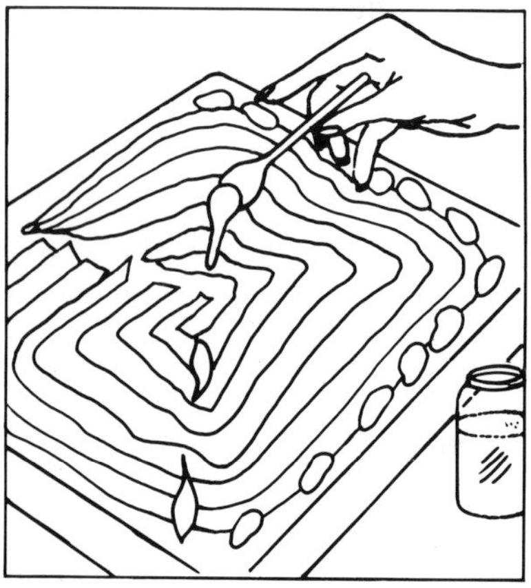

Fig 2 Tritik technique: dab a little fabric paint along the folds

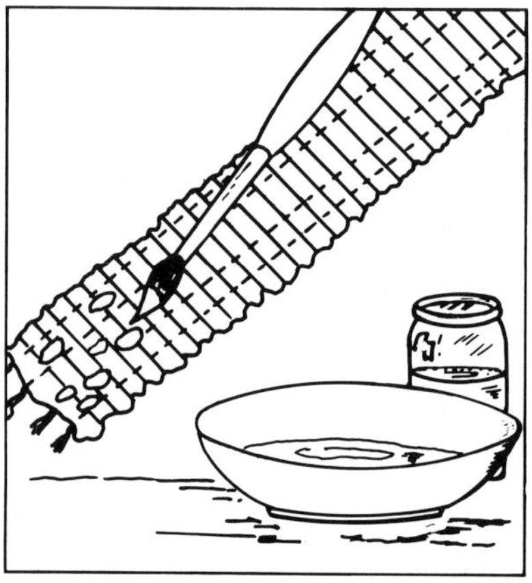

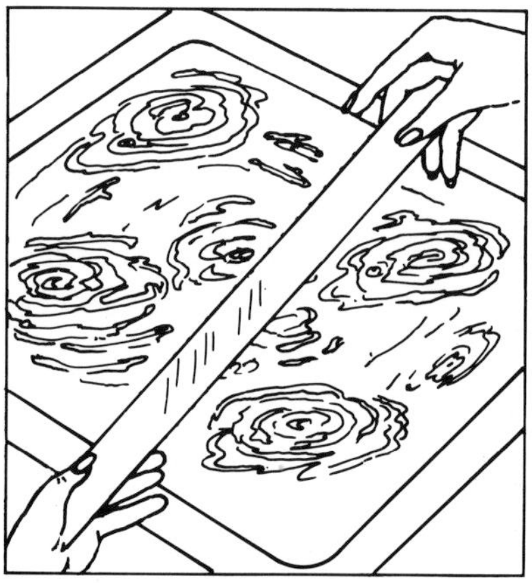

Fig 3 Marbling ribbons: lay ribbon on the surface of the marbling liquid

on the block and print again. Continue along the length of the ribbon. Leave it to dry. The colour will become slightly paler when it is dry. Wash the block and the brush clean and leave to dry.

When the first printing is completely dry, print the second colour and again leave the ribbon to dry.

When all printing has been completed, iron the ribbons to set the paint. Satin and taffeta ribbons print equally well.

Tritik ribbons

This is a method of making patterns on ribbons by gathering them very tightly and then painting the folds with fabric paint. The tightly drawn gathering prevents the paint from penetrating the folds, and the pattern is formed by the original colour of the ribbon separating the painted areas. (An example of this technique can be seen on the jacket of this book.)

Method

Using a sewing thread, work running stitches along both edges of the work two or three rows down the middle also, depending on the width of the ribbon. The lines of stitches should be about 1cm (⅜ in) apart. They can also be worked using a smock-gathering machine, or on a sewing machine using a long straight stitch. Pull up the gathering threads tightly, and knot them together at both ends.

Dilute the fabric paint to the texture of thin cream, and, using a paint-brush, dab a little paint at intervals along the top of the folds (Fig 2, page 12). If you use too much paint, or paint that is too runny, it will seep down between the folds and spoil the pattern. Dab on two or three colours in turn, allowing them to overlap each other. Some white spaces can be left between the colours. When all the folds on one side are coloured, turn the ribbon over and paint the other side. Allow to dry thoroughly.

Cut the gathering threads knots at one end and pull them out. Iron the ribbons to set the colours.

Marbling on ribbons

The best medium for marbling on ribbon is artists' oil paint, as fabric paints tend to result in too soft a pattern. Marbling can be done on a water base, but you will get better results if a caragheen moss size is used to float the colour. The moss, which is really a seaweed, can be obtained from craft shops and comes in a dried or a powdered form. (Make sure you buy the real thing and not a substitute.)

Water method

Pour 3cm (1¼ in) water into a flat dish. Thin artists' oil paint with white spirit to a consistency similar to ink. Mix each colour in a different pot. Using a paint brush, flick or gently drop paint onto the surface of the water. Different colours react in different ways – some spread thinly, some remain as droplets. Swirl the colours with a wooden toothpick and then quickly lay several lengths of ribbon on the surface of the water (Fig 3, page 12). Leave for a second or two so that the paint is absorbed, lift the ribbon off using both hands and lay it, paint side up, on old newspaper. Marble as many pieces of ribbon as required then wash them under cold running water and spread to dry on clean newspaper.

Caragheen moss method

Put 30g (1 oz) moss into a large saucepan and add 1 litre (1¾ pints) of cold water. Boil for 5 minutes. Strain the liquid through a fine sieve and discard the moss. Add another 1 litre (1¾ pints) of cold water and leave for 24 hours in a cool place. The size will keep for a further 2 days, or it can be frozen if you do not use it all at once. The size can be used as it is, or diluted with up to 3 times as much water. It must be used at room temperature.

Pour 3cm (1¼ in) of size into a flat dish. Mix artists' oil paints with white spirit until a consistency similar to ink. Using a paint brush, flick or drop colour onto the surface of the size allowing each colour to spread. Swirl into patterns with a feather or a comb. Lay the ribbons on the surface and leave for a few seconds. Lift them off and lay them, paint

side up, on newspaper. Wash the marbled ribbons under cold running water and spread on newspaper to dry.

Hints on marbling ribbons

If the paint sinks under the surface of the size, the paint is too thick and should be further diluted with white spirit. The colours should be thin enough to spread into a circle when dropped onto the size.

If too much paint is used, it will run off the ribbons and make a mess. The ideal amount is when it all gets picked up by the ribbons, and stays on them. If the surface of the size gets dirty, clean it by drawing a piece of absorbent kitchen paper across it.

For a different marbling effect, try thinning the oil paints with turpentine.

Rubbings with transfer crayons

These special crayons are not used directly on ribbons, but are used for drawing or rubbing on paper and are then ironed onto ribbons. The advantage of this technique is that multiple prints can be taken from one pattern. These crayons are designed for use on man-made fibres only (such as rayon, nylon or polyester).

Place a piece of thin drawing paper over a textured surface, such as a basket or some leaves. Rub over the paper with the crayons, changing the colour frequently. Cut the paper into strips the same width as the ribbon.

Place the strips, crayon side down, on the ribbons and iron over them at medium heat until the pattern is transferred. Move the paper strip along the ribbon and iron it again. When the crayonned strip is exhausted, use a new strip.

Enlarged detail of the bag pictured on page 63, made with space-dyed cotton knitting ribbon. The ribbon is woven through canvas covered with machine-satin stitch worked on each thread, changing the thread colour to keep paler tints at the top and deeper shades at the bottom

Stitching on ribbons

Decorating ribbons with stitchery can change the colour of a ribbon, add pattern or texture, or soften a too-strong existing pattern on the ribbon. Multiple lines of stitching along a ribbon, or one ribbon stitched along another, gives extra body and a beautiful handle. Stitching can be worked on any type of sewing machine.

Method

Thread the sewing machine with embroidery thread, either coloured or metallic. Using normal tension for both the bobbin and the top thread, stitch a row down the centre of the ribbon. Then stitch down the centre of the ribbon. Then stitch down the sides exactly on the selvedges. Continue, adding more rows of stitching until the ribbon is quite covered. The first rows of stitching will pucker the ribbon but as more rows are added it will lie flat again. As a guide, about 10 rows of stitching to 1cm (⅜ in) of width is the minimum.

If stitching is worked down one edge only you will notice that the stitching makes the ribbon curve. This could be a useful technique if a curved base for weaving is required. If stitching is worked down the centre of the ribbon only, it will flare at the edges, and this effect could be incorporated into an otherwise flat weaving to add texture. Two or three rows of stitching worked together look better than one.

Ribbons on ribbons

Laying one or more narrow ribbons on top of a wider ribbon and then stitching them together, gives an even richer look and handle. The narrow ribbon can be secured with zigzag or straight stitching, and more straight stitching added either side to fill in the spaces.

When stitched, ribbons tend to become slightly shorter, so allow an extra 7 - 8cm (2¾ - 3¾ in) for every 1m (1⅛ yd) needed. Twin needle stitching, incidentally, is not very successful. The ribbon seems to roll under and it does not lie flat enough.

CHAPTER TWO

Weaving methods and patterns

There are several different weaving methods which can be used in ribbon weaving and some are given here. The method you choose will depend on the item being made and its end use. Although the instructions for making the various projects on the following pages each suggest a particular method, you may prefer to substitute another that suits you better.

Because modern ribbons are fairly firm in texture a fabric made from weaving also tends to have a firm handle. The iron-on interfacing method described here produces the least flexible fabric while the softest result comes from weaving a pliable, tubular knitting ribbon through a soft mesh fabric.

It is always worth working small 15cm (6 in)-square samples to find the 'handle' you prefer for a particular project. If the first sample does not turn out to be quite right, then try another method, or use different ribbons. It is better to make mistakes at this early stage when they can be corrected, than after the article is finished.

Weaving on iron-on interfacing
1   Cut a piece of iron-on interfacing slightly larger than the finished size of the project. Pencil any shape or outline on the interfacing. Place it adhesive side upwards on a cork mat. Pin to the mat at the corners.
2   Cut the warp ribbons about 2.5cm (1 in) longer than needed and pin them, edges touching, through the interfacing into the board, 12mm (½ in) outside the top edge of the pencilled shape as shown in Fig 1. This 12mm (½ in) will form the seam allowance at the making-up stage. (Ribbons can be pinned down at both ends if you wish.) Note that pins should be set angled away from the

work. This helps to get the iron right up to the edges of the work at the pressing stage.
3   Cut the weft ribbons also a little longer than needed. Using the fingers (or a bodkin for very narrow ribbons) weave them horizontally through the warp ribbons, following the chosen weave. Pin the weft ribbons at both ends (Fig 2). Continue weaving until the pattern is completed, pinning down the ends of the warp ribbons, if this was not done earlier.
4   Dry-press over the woven ribbons from the right side using a medium hot iron. Press until you are sure that the ribbons have adhered. Remove the pins, turn the work over and press again, on an ironing board, over a damp cloth. Allow to dry. The ribbons will have bonded to the interfacing and thus a fabric has been produced that can be cut and stitched, just as any other fabric. It is often used for items which are likely to receive a lot of wear, such as cushion covers, or where complex shapes are to be cut from the weaving.

Weaving backed with a fabric
In this method, the ribbons are pinned over a piece of fabric.

1   Cut a piece of fabric (cotton, calico or lining fabric, depending on the end use of the item) and pin it to a cork mat at the corners. Pencil any shape or outline on the fabric.
2   Cut warp and weft ribbons as for the iron-on interfacing technique, and pin and weave the ribbons.
3   When weaving is completed, remove the pins one by one and re-pin the ribbons to the fabric only (Fig 3). Baste all round, remove the pins, then machine-stitch the edges to

hold the ribbons. This method results in a softer fabric, with the fabric holding the weaving in place and acting as a lining as well. This method is usually used when making garments or insets for garments from ribbon weaving. It can also be used for textured ribbon weaving that would not be ironed.

Backed weaving on a frame

This method involves the use of a rectangular embroidery frame or a picture frame. An artist's stretcher can also be used.

1 Draw the outline or pattern shape on a piece of calico, then pin the calico into the frame using drawing pins, stretching it taut.
2 Cut and pin the warp ribbons to the calico following the outline of the pattern. Cut the weft ribbons and weave through the warp, pinning the ends.
3 When weaving is completed, remove the fabric from the frame, removing the pins one by one, and baste the edges.

This method can be used when you wish to hand-stitch ribbons to a backing to make a firmer fabric such as when making cushion covers, seat covers, wall panels etc.

You can also use the frame technique for hand-quilting ribbon weaving. After pinning the backing fabric, lay wadding over the top and then weave the ribbon. Quilt the weaving on the frame.

Un-backed weaving

The same basic technique can be used without the backing fabric. Pin the warp ribbons

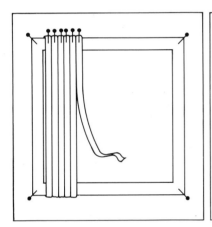

Fig 1   Pin the warp ribbons edge to edge, 12mm (½ in) over pattern line

Fig 2   Weft ribbons in an over 1, under 1 weave, pinned both ends

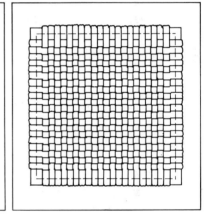

Fig 3   Pin ribbons to the backing fabric, then baste, removing pins

Fig 4   Pin warp and weft ribbons to frame-mounted calico backing

Fig 5   Weaving on a nail board: weave weft ribbons with a needle

Fig 6   Weaving over canvas: warp and weft ribbons lie on the canvas

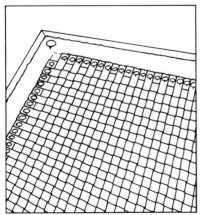

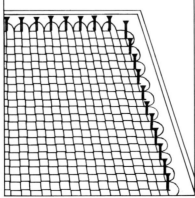

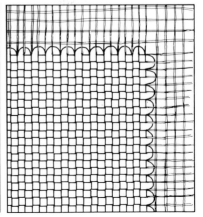

to two opposite sides of the frame. Pin the weft ribbons to the other two sides as you weave. Then pin the warp and weft ribbons together as the weaving is removed from the frame. Baste, then work zigzag machine-stitch round the edges to secure the weaving.

Alternative method
Another variation is to pin the warp and weft ribbons to the cork mat with no backing of any kind. When the weaving is complete, re-pin the warp ribbons to the weft ribbons round the edges, lift from the cork mat and baste, removing the pins. Zigzag machine-stitch to secure the edges of the weaving. This method is a little tricky to handle, but the resulting weaving is softer than either of the two previous methods.

Weaving on a nail board
1   Draw the outline of the shape to be woven on paper. Pin it to a nail board.
2   Hammer oval nails about 2.5cm (1 in) apart round the outline. Tie the end of a single

length of narrow ribbon to the first nail. Take it across to an opposite nail and round once. Continue winding backwards and forwards across the board making a weft.
3   Weave the weft ribbon through the warp, winding it round the nails at the beginning and end of every row (Fig 5 page 17).
4   When the weaving is finished, carefully lift it off the nails. You have made a piece of weaving which can be applied to another fabric or used as it is.

Weaving over canvas
This method is similar to the nail board method, except that the warp ribbons are threaded through the canvas at the top and bottom edges of an outlined shape.

Right: Plain, under 1, over 1 weave using a warp of wide, printed ribbons and a weft of narrower plain satin and machine-stitched ribbons
Below: Three-layered weave with the weft in an under 1, over 2 weave, each row staggered 1 ribbon to the left. Three narrow ribbons are then woven diagonally in an under 1, over 1 weave

1 You will need single thread canvas with 10 holes to 2.5cm (1 in) or a larger mesh, depending on the width of the ribbons. Thread the end of the warp ribbon into a large-eyed needle and pass it through the canvas, under a vertical thread then bring it through to the right side again. Secure the end with a knot.

2 Take the warp ribbon across the canvas, under the same vertical thread, then bring it through to the right side. Continue in the same way, completing the warp.

3 Weave the weft ribbons through the warp ribbons only, above the surface of the canvas but passing the needle through the canvas at the both sides of the weaving. This method covers the canvas and is quicker to do than weaving through every hole (Fig 6 page 17).

Weaving through net and mesh fabrics

In this method the ribbons are woven in only one direction, and are taken over and under the threads of the base fabric, becoming part of it. Thread narrow ribbon into a bodkin or a large-eyed, blunt-tipped needle. Needleweave the ribbon up and down through the holes of the base fabric. Work with the fabric flat on the table. Needleweaving can be worked through single holes or two or three holes together. The type of fabric being used will dictate which kind of stitch is worked. To avoid the ribbon constantly twisting, hold the loop of ribbon with the thumb and forefinger while the right (or working) hand pulls the needle and ribbon through. You will need to untwist the ribbon occasionally. The easiest way to do this is to lay the work on a table, lift the ribbon with the needle hanging on the end and let it untwirl.

Patterns for ribbon weaving

Although most of the projects in this book use a simple under 1, over 1 pattern, there are many more weaves that can be worked. A few are illustrated here and on pages 22-23. Some are simple, some are complex, but they can all be varied using the elements of colour, ribbon width and spacing. Different textures can be mixed, such as matt ribbons

Fig 1 This is the simplest weave of all, an under 1 over 1 pattern. It can be worked with the ribbon edges touching to make a close-textured fabric, or the ribbons can be spaced. The sample illustrated here shows the effect of ribbons with coloured edges.

Fig 4 This is the same weave as Fig 3 but alternate ribbons of the warp here are different colours, and so are alternate rows of the weft. This is a good example of the possible variations by using colours in a different order.

20

Fig 2 A development of the under 1, over 1 pattern worked with narrow ribbons of all the same width. An open pattern such as this could also be worked over a backing of a plain coloured fabric.

Fig 3 To work this pattern, set an odd number of warp ribbons. Weave the 1st row under 2, over 2. For row 2, weave over 1, then under 2, over 2 to the end. Row 3 begins with over 2, then under 2. Row 4 begins under 1, then over 2. Repeat rows 1 – 4.

Fig 5 This is stage 1 of the same weave, showing the warp ribbons set diagonally. In **Fig 6**, the effect of the weave can be seen, using the same weaving pattern described for Fig 3. The herringbone effect can be striking if strongly contrasting ribbons are used or can

be subtle with closely-toning shades. The weave is close in texture and is thus very suitable for weaving fabric for home furnishings and for fashion garments and accessories. The weave works well with very narrow ribbons also.

with shiny ones, smooth with ribbed surfaces, velvet with satin, and thus dozens of different effects are possible.

Ideas for weaving patterns are all around you; there are the patterns in woven rush and cane chair seats, in basket weaves, in fences and in woven fabrics. A woven fabric looked at through a magnifying glass, will show the structure in detail with the number of over-and-under movements providing a source of different patterns. Weaving and plaiting patterns from textiles of other cultures will also provide inspiration. Sketch these from books or from museum collections so that you have a record and thus you can build up a collection of ideas which can be altered and adapted to make even more patterns for your ribbon weaving.

Choosing the weaving method
It is extremely important to choose the weaving method that will give you the best results for your purpose. Each has advantages and disadvantages which should be considered when planning work.

The iron-on interfacing method is a good general-purpose one, but the finished fabric can be too stiff. Weaving over canvas works well for articles that need body, such as cushions, but it is too bulky a fabric for light-weight articles. Weaving through nets gives a pliable result, good for clothes, scarves and shawls, but the fabric is too soft for items such as stool tops or chair seats. Weaving on a fabric backing produces a pliable fabric with some body but if shapes are to be cut from it, it requires special preparation (see shaped pieces page 24).

Fig 7

Fig 7 a very simple weave achieved by setting the warp ribbons horizontally and then weaving the weft ribbons on the diagonal. Small spaces show between the ribbons here but a close texture can be worked if preferred. **Fig 8** Another simple over 1, under 1 weave

Fig 10

between, then weave vertical ribbons under 1 over 1 on horizontal ribbons only with spaces between. Lay diagonal ribbons from top right to bottom left under diagonal ribbons, over straight. **Fig 11** Lay horizontal ribbons with wide spaces, then the vertical ribbons with

Fig 8

Fig 9

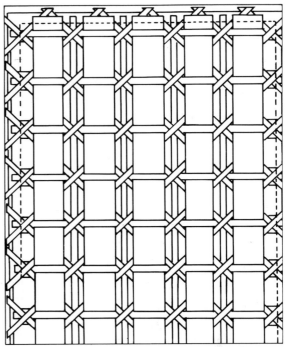

using wide ribbons with very narrow ribbons woven through on the diagonal in an under 1, over 2 pattern.
Fig 9 This is a Japanese 5-layer pattern; to weave, lay wide horizontal warp ribbons with spaces between. Lay wide vertical ribbons with spaces, then weave narrow

ribbons from top left to bottom right under wide and over narrow. Then weave narrow ribbons from top right to bottom left under wide and over narrow.
Fig 10 Lay diagonal ribbons from top left to bottom right. Lay narrow horizontal ribbons with space

Fig 11

Fig 12

wide spaces weaving under 1, over 1. Weave the diagonals from top right to bottom left over horizontals and under verticals with spaces between. Weave the diagonals from top left to bottom right under the verticals and over horizontals. **Fig 12** is a development

of the pattern with 2 ribbons laid side by side horizontally and vertically, woven through each other at intersections. Next, lay diagonals from top left to bottom right under horizontals and over verticals and the opposite diagonal over horizontals and under verticals

Making up woven articles

When the woven ribbon fabric is finished, it is then ready to make up into an article, and there are various ways of doing this. First, the woven fabric must be kept on the straight grain while being woven and when preparing to make it up. If the ribbons waver and depart from the straight the finished article will look unsightly. This distortion can happen sometimes with the iron-on interfacing method (page 16), when the heat of the iron distorts the weave. If this occurs, carefully lift the ribbons, peel them from the backing, replace them in the right place, pin to secure and press again. However, distortion is not usually a problem with any of the other methods.

If you are weaving without iron-on interfacing, the ribbon ends must be secured first so that the weaving does not fall apart. Pin each ribbon end to the ribbon underneath it, working all round the edges. Baste the ribbons together on the pin line, remove the pins and work 2 rows of stitching 6mm (¼ in) apart using either a straight machine-stitch, or a zigzag machine-stitch (Fig 1). Then cut out on the basted line. You can sew the ribbons together by hand using running stitch if you prefer. If the ribbon ends seem particularly fragile, stitch them to a piece of tape to strengthen them (Fig 2). You cannot risk the whole thing coming apart while you are making it up, so make sure everything is secure at this stage.

Shaped pieces

If a shaped piece is to be cut from the weaving place the pattern piece on top, pin and then baste all round. This is the cutting line (Fig 3). Remove the pattern piece and work 2 rows of machine stitching 6mm (¼ in) apart,

either side of the cutting line. Then cut out the shape (Fig 4).

Narrow ribbons

The ends of the very narrow ribbons are not as easy to secure as the wider ones. After weaving, hold them in place at the ends with strips of sticky tape, then stitch tape to the edges of the weaving.

Finishing edges

There are various ways of finishing edges, depending on what you are making. If the edges are hidden within a seam, then zigzag machine-stitch will prevent the seam edges from ravelling. If the edge is on the outside, it can be finished with bias-cut binding (see Fig 5), which is particularly good for quilted articles. Commercially-made satin bias binding can also be used. Ribbon should not be used for binding as this tends to wrinkle and it is difficult to turn corners neatly.

Making up

Making up items from ribbon weaving using a sewing machine presents no problems. Use a medium-length straight stitch, at normal sewing tension. If extra strength is required, 3 rows of straight stitch, worked close together, could be used. If hand-sewing is preferred, use a firm back-stitch, starting and finishing thread ends with a double back-stitch so that they do not come undone.

Some weaves, particularly those where a ribbon travels over two or more ribbons, may need extra strengthening and to achieve this the fabric can be quilted by stitching between the lines of ribbon through a wadding and a backing fabric.

Quilting looks good for articles such as bed

covers, jackets, needle and jewellery rolls and cases, mats, pot covers, bags and cushions etc but it is usually too bulky for items such as books and file covers (Refer to page 37 for quilting techniques.) Alternatively, if the weaving has been worked over a lining or backing fabric, stitch between the lines of the ribbons and through the backing. The resulting fabric is, of course, slightly stiffer but it is ideal for items where only a little extra body is required, such as a bolero jacket or waistcoat.

If preferred, edges can be finished with satin stitch worked on a sewing machine. Set the machine to a medium-width zigzag stitch, and a very short stitch length. Work one row along the edge at this width, then cover it with another row at a slightly wider width, then a third row at the full width of the zigzag stitch (Fig 6). For a hand finish, work a close buttonhole stitch on raw edges.

Fig 1   Baste ribbon ends on the pin line then work 2 row of machine-stitching. Cut out on the basting line

Fig 2   Stitch cotton tape along the edges of fragile ribbon weaving to strengthen it

Fig 3   Pin pattern to finished weaving and baste all round

Fig 4   After machine-stitching either side of the basting line, cut out on the basting line

Fig 5   To neaten edges, stitch bias binding right sides facing then slipstitch binding on the wrong side

Fig 6   Work 2 rows of machine-zigzag stitch, then finish with close satin stitch to neaten edges

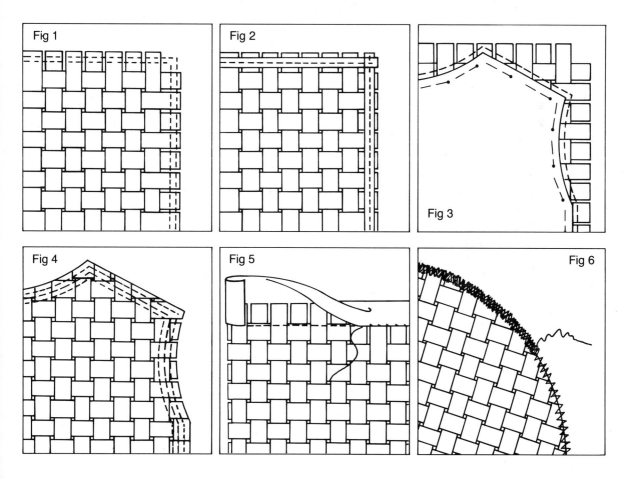

CHAPTER THREE

Weaving ribbons through ribbons

The effect of ribbons woven through other ribbons has almost endless variations of pattern and colour. The resulting fabric is fairly firm and can be made up into bags, cushions, details on clothes, jackets and waistcoats, small accessories such as wallets, notebook covers and spectacles cases, baby quilts, picture frames and boxes.

Weaving satin or taffeta ribbons alone produces a rich luxurious-looking fabric but this is not always what is required for a specific project. Include some matt cotton ribbons, or delicate net ribbons or velvet ribbons to vary the texture and a different fabric effect will result. Different types of ribbon are worth experimenting with also – picot and looped-edge ribbons make interesting patterns when woven with smooth-edged ribbons.

Twelve pattern ideas for weaving ribbons through ribbons are given on pages 20-21, 22-23 and you will find it worthwhile trying these out before working projects with them.

As you experiment with different colours and textures you will almost certainly evolve new patterns and these will add individuality to your work.

Painting, printing and stitching on ribbons adds individuality and techniques and ideas for decorating ribbons can be found in Chapter One, pages 10-15.

Quality ribbons can be expensive when a large piece of weaving is being considered. Try including the less expensive knitting ribbons and tapes, or use cut or torn strips of fabric pieces or raffia, to reduce the cost, as well as providing texture.

When planning a piece of weaving, consider the different widths of ribbon available, and combine narrow and wide ribbons together in the same piece. Narrow ribbons can be used alone, laid along wider ribbons or three lengths can be plaited together and used as a single length. A weaving pattern will look quite different when woven with ribbons all of the same width, and then with ribbons in at least two different widths, even if the same colour scheme is used. Before starting on a project, it is worth buying short lengths of ribbons and making small samples to try various colour combinations.

Ribbons through ribbons projects
In this chapter, there are instructions for making some pretty accessories, a baby quilt and jacket, a velvet ribbon cushion, two garden cushions, a file cover and a burse, a breakfast set and ribbon neckties all using fabrics produced by weaving ribbons through ribbons. It is possible to use different weaves from those specified and, of course, different ribbons can be used. The more you experiment, the more individual will be the finished piece.

Right: Narrow metallic ribbons and stuffed tubular metallic ribbon knotted through the weave

Pretty ribbon accessories

Small ribbon-woven accessories are reasonably quick to work, and make very acceptable gifts for birthdays, anniversaries or for festive occasions. All kinds of things can be made – belts and headbands, spectacles and sun glasses cases, needlebooks, needle rolls and scissor cases, bags and purses, file covers, book covers and cheque book covers, slippers, shoe bags – the list is almost endless. For co-ordinated gift sets, bands of ribbon weaving can be stitched to the ends of plain coloured towels, with matching toilet bags or handkerchief holders, or to the edges of tray-cloths, matched to napkin rings or pot covers. Remember that if items are to be laundered, washable, colourfast ribbons must be used and it is advisable to choose polyester ribbons. (See picture page 31.)

Spectacles case

The inspiration for this colour scheme came from seeing a terracotta statue against lilac suede in an Italian museum – a reminder of the importance of keeping notes of what you see.

Materials required

2 pieces of lining fabric 11 × 16cm (4½ × 6½ in)
9 × 16cm (3½ × 6¼ in) piece of thick card
11cm × 34cm (4½ × 13½ in) piece of pelmetweight interfacing
Car spray paint to tone with the ribbons
Sewing thread
A mixture of velvet and satin ribbons in different colours in the following widths:
8m (8¾ yd) of 1.5m (¹⁄₁₆ in)-wide ribbon (for warp and tassels)
38cm (15 in) of 15mm (⁵⁄₈ in)-wide ribbon

76cm (30½ in) of 9mm (³⁄₈ in)-wide ribbon
3m (3¼ yd) of 1.5mm (¹⁄₁₆ in)-wide ribbon
1.50m (1⁵⁄₈ yd) of 6mm (¼ in)-wide ribbon

Preparation

1   Make up the lining by stitching the 2 pieces together on long sides and one short side, right sides facing.
2   Fold the interfacing over the piece of card and pin on the long edges. Baste, then machine-stitch the seams, using the machine's zipper foot so that you can stitch close to the edges of the card. Trim the seams close to the stitching.
3   Spray the interfacing case with car spray paint, covering the edges.
4   Using a felt-tipped pen, measure and mark off at 6mm (¼ in) intervals down both long sides of the case.

Weaving

5   Sew one end of the very narrow warp ribbon to the top right corner of the case. Wind the end round the case, so that the ribbon lies on the marks on each edge (Fig 1). Do not wind too tightly. Sew the end of the ribbon to the bottom corner. Trim off any excess ribbon.
6   Cut all the ribbons into 38cm (15 in) lengths.
7   Using a long bodkin, weave each length of ribbon in turn through the narrow ribbon warp, starting at the top edge, working down to the base, turning the case over and working up the other side. Leave the ribbon ends protruding at the top edge. Push each ribbon close to the one preceding.
8   Remove the card stiffening from the case. Fold the ribbon ends to the inside and pin in place. Sew them to the interfacing.

9 Drop the prepared lining into the case, pushing the bottom corners down with a ruler. Turn a hem to the wrong side, pin, baste and sew with hemming or slipstitches.

10 Make two small tassels (refer to page 81) and sew them to the top corners.

Needle roll

Most needlebooks are far too small to be practical, and it is difficult to see which needle is needed at a glance. Needle rolls are an alternative way of keeping needles organised, and could be adapted to make a sewing case. The roll pictured is woven from satin and taffeta ribbons which have been sponge painted, then printed with a star-shaped rubber stamp. The stars were drawn over with a silver marker to provide definition. Some ribbons were streaked with silver glitter fabric paint, and others stitched with metallic machine-embroidery threads.

Materials required

4m (4⅜ yd) of 9mm (⅜ in)-wide ribbon
4m (4⅜ yd) of 12mm (½ in)-wide ribbon
1 reel metallic machine-embroidery thread
Machine sewing thread
25cm (10 in) square of felt
1m (1⅛ yd) bias binding (optional)

Preparation

1 In the roll pictured, the warp ribbons were painted and printed first. The felt for lining was also painted with fabric paint. Some of the narrower, weft ribbons were overstitched with metallic machine-embroidery thread.

2 On the adhesive side of the interfacing, pencil a 20cm (8 in) square. Pin the interfacing to a cork mat.

3 Cut the warp ribbons 22cm (8½ in) long, retaining 75cm (30 in) of 9mm (⅜ in)-wide ribbon for ties. Pin the ribbons, edges touching, along the top and bottom edges of the marked area.

4 Using a plain weave, weave the weft ribbons, pinning on both edges..

5 Bond the weaving to the interfacing (refer to page 16) and remove the pins.

6 Pin the finished weaving to the piece of felt.

7 Quilt the fabric by machine-stitching between the warp ribbons.

8 Stitch round the edges of the weaving and trim away the excess ribbon ends, close to the stitching.

9 Cut the reserved ribbon into 2 pieces and pin, then sew in the centre of one side edge for ties.

10 To finish, work 2 rows of machine satin stitch all round. Needles etc are inserted into the felt lining. Roll up and fasten with the ribbon ties.

Fig 1 Wind the narrow ribbon round the interfacing case, on the marked points

Fig 2 Plan the jewellery roll with pockets and holders as required. Ribbons hold rings, earrings and earclips

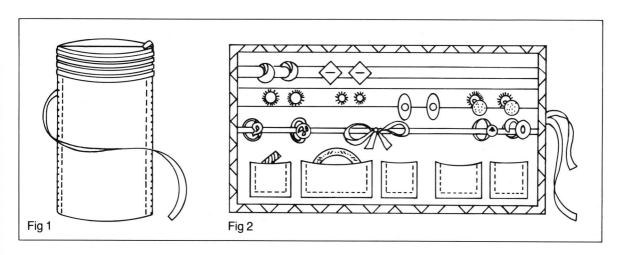

Fig 1   Fig 2

Jewellery roll

A jewellery roll can be made in the same way to keep jewellery secure when travelling. Rolls are not very good for bulky necklaces or bracelets but are quite useful for delicate pieces.

Making a jewellery roll

1 Prepare a piece of weaving 40 × 20cm (16 × 8 in).
2 Cut a piece of satin fabric to the same size.
3 Lay out the jewellery intended to be kept in the roll, and plan pockets and holders as required (Fig 2, page 29).
4 Make pockets by cutting squares or rectangles of satin, then turn and press narrow hems on all four sides. Stitch one edge. Pin in position, then stitch on the 3 remaining sides, sew press fasteners to close the pockets.
5 For rings, lay 2 ribbons across the width, sewing one end to the lining edges (see Fig 2). The rings are slipped onto the ribbons and the ends tied in a bow.
6 Sew 1 piece of ribbon to both edges of the fabric. Fasten earclips to the ribbon. For pierced ear earrings, sew 2 pieces of ribbon together on the selvedges, then work eyelets through both thicknesses. Sew the ribbons to the lining edges.
7 Finish the jewellery roll as for the needle roll, sewing ribbon ties on one short edge.

Handkerchief sachet

Handkerchief sachets are a graceful idea from the past but they are still a practical way of protecting fine handkerchiefs in a drawer. The sachet is made like an envelope. Three corners of a square are brought to the middle and sewn together. The fourth corner forms the sachet flap.

Materials required

1.40m (1½ yd) of 15mm (⅝ in)-wide lilac satin ribbon, A
1.40m (1½ yd) of 15mm (⅝ in)-wide rose pink satin ribbon, B
1.70m (1⅞ yd) of 25mm (1 in)-wide white satin ribbon, C
3m (3¼ yd) of 15mm (⅝ in)-wide pink satin ribbon, D
1.40m (1½yd) of 3mm (⅛ in)-wide lilac satin ribbon, E
1.40m (1½ yd) of 6mm (¼ in)-wide orchid satin ribbon, F
56cm (22 in) of 9mm (⅜ in)-wide pink satin ribbon, G
4m (4⅜ yd) of 1.5mm (1/16 in)-wide rose pink satin ribbon, H
110cm (43 in) of narrow silver ric-rac braid
1 reel silver machine-embroidery thread
1 reel blue, pink and silver variegated machine-embroidery thread
26cm (10½ in) square of iron-on interfacing
26cm (10½ in) square of bonding web
26cm (10½ in) square of lining fabric
Fabric paints as required

Preparation

1 Decorate the white ribbon, C, by any of the methods described on pages 10-13, using printing, sponging or the tritik method. Allow to dry, and iron to fix the fabric paint.
2 Machine-stitch the lilac ribbon, A, with silver thread. Work 16 to 18 rows of stitching across the width of the ribbon, until it lies flat, without puckering.
3 Machine-stitch the pink satin ribbon, B, using the variegated metallic thread, in the same way.
4 Lay the iron-on interfacing, adhesive side up, on a cork mat or pin board, and lay the card square in the centre of it. Measure and draw a 25cm (10 in) square on the interfacing.
5 Cut the decorated white ribbon and the pink B ribbon into 6 27cm (10¾ in) lengths.
6 Pin the ribbons, alternating, across the drawn pattern. Pin at both ends.
7 Cut the stitched ribbons, A and B into 27cm (10¾ in) lengths, and weave them, together with the plain D, E, F and G ribbons. Any weaving pattern from pages 20-21, 22-23 can be used, or use a plain weave in a random colour scheme, as shown in the picture.
8 Bond the finished weaving to the interfacing (refer to page 16).
9 Cut and weave lengths of the silver ric-rac

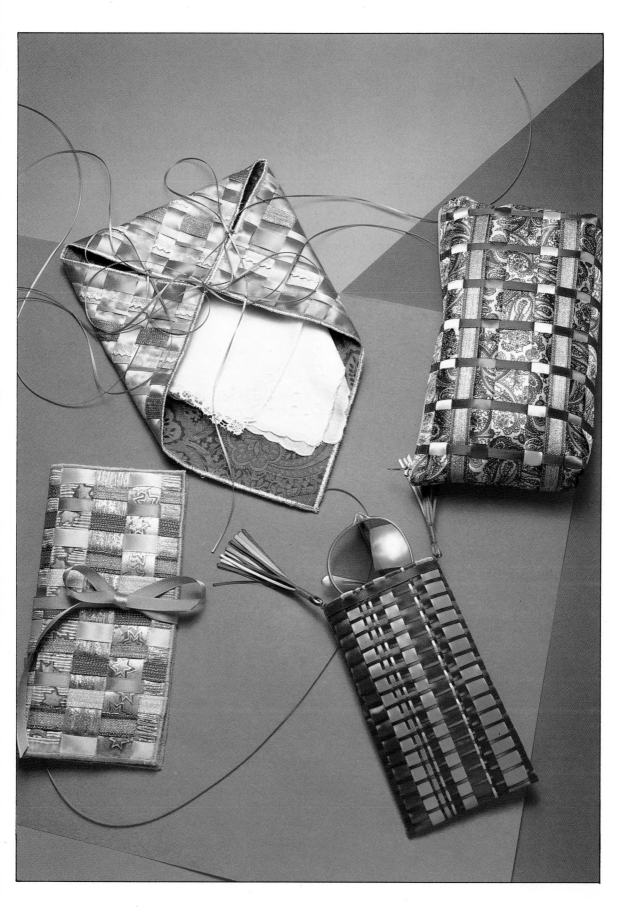

braid through the weaving (see picture) on top of the silver-stitched lilac (A) ribbons. Pin at the edges to secure. Turn the woven fabric over and press again on the wrong side.

10   Iron the bonding web onto the wrong side of the lining fabric. Allow to cool.

11   Lay the weaving right side down on the cork mat. Peel the paper backing from the bonding web on the lining. Place the lining, web-side down on the weaving. Press firmly to bond weaving to lining.

12   Machine-stitch around the edges of the weaving, near to the outer edge of the ribbons. Trim ribbon ends close to the stitching.

13   Cut the 1.5mm (1/16 in)-wide ribbon (H) into 8 pieces. Pin one piece of ribbon at each corner of the square. Pin pieces of ribbon 5cm (2 in) each side of corners b, c and d (see diagram, Fig 3). Sew or machine-stitch the ribbons in place.

14   Work machine satin stitch at width 2 round the edge of the square using silver thread. Stitch again at width 3, and then again at width 4.

15   Hold points b and d together so that they touch and sew together using a figure-of-eight movement so that the points lie flat. Bring up point c and sew it to b and d to make the sachet pocket.

16   Tie the ribbons at b and d together and knot them. Knot the ribbons at each side of b and d also. Ribbons a and c are tied loosely to hold the handkerchiefs in place.

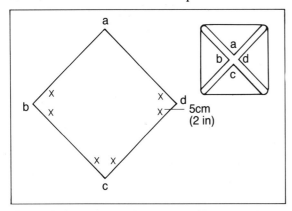

Fig 3   To fasten the sachet, tie the ribbons together at b and d, then knot the ribbons at each side of b and d. Ribbons a and c are loosely tied

Case for cosmetics

Here, paisley-patterned ribbon has been combined with stitched plain satin ribbons.

Materials required

4.50m (4⅞ yd) of 25mm (1 in)-wide paisley-patterned ribbon (A)
2.50m (2¾ yd) of 6mm (¼ in)-wide satin ribbon (B)
3.90m (4¼ yd) of 12mm (½ in)-wide satin ribbon (C)
1.20m (1⅜ yd) of 15mm (⅝ in)-wide satin ribbon (D)
1 reel metallic machine-embroidery thread
Matching sewing thread
20cm (8 in)-long zip fastener
25 × 32cm (10 × 12½ in) piece of lining fabric
25 × 32cm (10 × 12½ in) piece of iron-on interfacing

Preparation

1   Cut 1.20m (1⅜ yd) of ribbon C and 1.20m (1⅜ yd) of ribbon D. Lay C on D and machine-stitch together on the long edges. (The remaining C ribbon can also be machine-stitched if desired.)

2   Draw 2 rectangles 15 × 23.5cm (6 × 9½ in) on the iron-on interfacing.

Weaving

3   Using a plain weave and referring to the picture, weave the front and back of the case. Finish the weaving as described on page 16.

4   Machine-stitch the edges of the weaving, then trim back to the stitching line.

5   Fold one long edge on each piece 12mm (½ in) to the wrong side and pin.

6   On one piece, pin and baste the folded edge along one side of the zip's teeth. Do the same with the other side. Machine-stitch close to the fold edge, working 2 rows of stitching.

7   Open the zip. Fold the bag with the right sides together. Pin, baste and machine-stitch on three sides, leaving a 6mm (¼ in) seam allowance and curving the corners.

8   Make up the lining, drop it into the bag, turn in the top edge and hem to the inside edges of the bag, just below the zip.

Belts, bands, beads and buttons

Ribbon-woven fashion accessories enable you to make items in co-ordinated colour schemes. A belt, for instance, can be worked in colours matched to the dress fabric, with perhaps a purse or a hair-band in the same ribbon colours. Hair bows and neck bows for shirts or blouses are made from a straight piece of lined weaving, made up and sewn to a clip or pin. Soft jewellery is another fashion idea for ribbon work. Pendants, bracelets and chokers can be woven in lurex ribbons, perhaps embellished with beads and sequins. Wooden beads, covered with ribbon, make bright, ethnic-looking jewellery or fastenings. For an individual finish on hand-made clothes, cover button moulds with weaving made with very narrow ribbons or needle-woven fabric.

Belts

Tie belts are made from a straight strip of ribbon weaving, stiffened with pelmet-weight interfacing and lined with fabric.

Preparation

1   Measure the waist and decide the width of the belt. Draw an area to the measurements on iron-on interfacing. Pin the interfacing to a cork mat.

Weaving

2   Cut warp ribbons to the belt's length plus 2.5cm (1 in) for seam allowance. Pin the ribbons at both ends.
3   Cut the weft ribbons to the depth of the belt plus 2.5cm (1 in) for seam allowance. Weave and pin the ribbons.
4   Bond the weaving to the interfacing (see page 16) and remove the pins.
5   Machine-stitch all round 9mm (3/8 in) from the drawn pattern line. Cut out just outside the line of stitching.   ▶

Fig 1   Tie belt fastened with ribbons

Fig 2   Narrow belt fastened with a bead and ribbon loop

Fig 3   Cover the bead with a thread warp (a) then needleweave narrow ribbon through the threads (b)

Fig 4   Beads can also be covered with 6mm (1/4 in)-wide ribbons without a warp

Fig 5   Cover button moulds with ribbon weaving, or with fabric for needleweaving

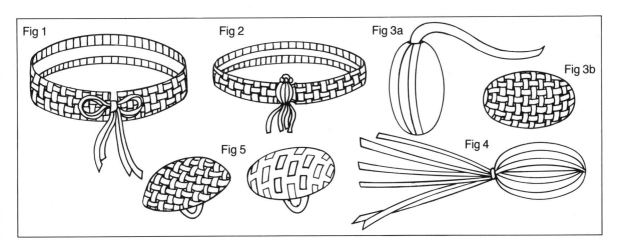

6 Cut a piece of interfacing to the belt's dimensions. Lay the interfacing on the wrong side of the weaving and fold the edges of the weaving onto the interfacing. Pin, baste and press.

7 Catch the weaving edges to the interfacing with lacing stitches.

8 Cut narrow ribbons for ties (three or four lengths look pretty). Sew the ties together to the interfacing at the belt ends.

9 Cut a piece of lining fabric to the belt's length and width measurements plus 12mm (½ in) for turnings. Press the turnings to the wrong side.

10 Sew the lining to the back of the belt using slip stitches (Fig 1, page 33).

Alternative fastening

For a bead and loop fastening, sew a loop of narrow ribbon to each end of the belt, slipping a covered bead on the left hand loop, before sewing in the lining (Fig 2, page 33).

Covered beads

A yarn warp is put onto the bead first.

1 Thread a long needle with fine, strong yarn or thread. Glue the end inside the bead and then wind the thread over the bead so that the threads lie about 1.5mm (¹⁄₁₆ in) apart. There should be an odd number. Glue the thread end to the inside (Fig 3a, page 33).

Weaving

2 Thread a needle with 1.5mm (¹⁄₁₆ in)-wide ribbon. Glue the end to the bead, tucking it under the threads.

Weave the ribbon through the threads in an under 1, over 1 weave to cover the bead. Glue the ribbon end to the bead (Fig 3b). For an alternative method and using a 6mm (¼ in)-wide ribbon, wind the ribbon over the bead, leaving the ends hanging. Tie the ends together (Fig 4, page 33).

Covered buttons

Button moulds can be covered with a fabric made from ribbon weaving using 3mm (⅛ in) ribbons. Alternatively, cover the button mould with a piece of even-weave fabric, such as linen, and then needleweave narrow ribbons through the fabric (Fig 5, page 33).

Quilted baby jacket and coverlet

Close quilting means that the ribbon-woven jacket can be machine-washed and yet it is pretty enough to be worn on special occasions. If preferred, the underarm and side seams can be seamed and the fronts fastened with buttonhole loops and small buttons.

The coverlet pictured opposite measures 56 × 68cm (22 × 27 in) but could be made larger for a cot.

Materials required for the Jacket

To fit a baby 6 - 12 weeks old:
Squared dressmaker's paper, scale 1 square = 2.5cm (1 in)
75cm (30 in) square piece of soft iron-on interfacing
20m (22 yd) of 25mm (1 in)-wide ribbons, single-faced satin and taffeta
1.40m (1½ yd) of 120cm (48 in)-wide lining fabric
75cm (30 in) square piece of 50g (2 oz) polyester wadding
7.50m (8¼ yd) of 3mm (⅛ in)-wide ribbon
1 reel of variegated machine-embroidery thread.
3m (3¼ yd) of satin bias binding (or bias-cut fabric)

Preparation

1 Draw the pattern from Fig 1, page 36 on squared paper. Glue the pattern to thin card and cut out the shape for a template.

2 Place the template on the adhesive side of the interfacing and trace round. Pin the interfacing to a cork mat.

3 Cut the 25mm (1 in)-wide ribbons for the warp and weft, adding 2.5cm (1 in) to each length for seam allowance. ▶

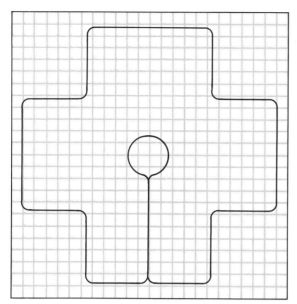

Fig 1   Graph pattern for the baby jacket, scale 1 sq =
2.5cm (1 in)

4   Weave the ribbons in an under 1, over 1
pattern, pinning the ends to the cork mat.
5   Bond the ribbons to the interfacing (refer
to page 16 for the technique).
6   Now prepare the weaving for quilting,
following the instructions on page 37.
7   Quilt in diagonal lines, using the corners
of the woven squares as a guide (see picture).
Quilt with machine-stitching, or by hand
using running stitches.
8   When the quilting is completed, spread
the quilting right side down and place the
card template on the lining. Draw round the
shape with a soft pencil.
9   Machine-stitch just inside the drawn line.
Trim back to the stitching through all layers.

Finishing

10   Cut the 1.5mm (¹⁄₁₆ in)-wide ribbons
into 20cm (8 in) lengths. Pin and baste in
pairs at 5cm (2 in) intervals down the front
edges and along the underarm and side
seams.
11   Bind all the jacket edges (refer to page
25 for binding techniques).
12   Sear the ends of the narrow ribbons with
a lighted match, to prevent fraying. Knot, or
tie the ribbons in bows, to join the underarm
and side seams

Varying the design

The underarm and side seams could also be
joined with insertion stitches after binding
the edges.
    Instead of an all-white scheme, vary the
colours by using yellow, peach and grey
ribbons together, or mid-blue, lime green
and bright pink.

Coverlet

The quantities given will make a coverlet 56
× 68cm (22 × 27 in). To make a coverlet for
a baby's cot or basket, add 20cm (8 in) to the
length measurement and 40cm (16 in) to the
width. You will need to re-estimate the
ribbon and fabric quantities and advice about
this is given on page 98 under *Estimating for
square and rectangular pieces.*

Materials required

For a coverlet 56 × 68cm (22 × 27 in):
*56 × 68cm (22 × 27 in) piece of soft iron-on
    interfacing*
*22.50m (24⅝ yd) of 25mm (1 in)-wide white
    or cream ribbon, some single-faced satin,
    some taffeta*
*2.75m (3 yd) of 77mm (3 in)-wide satin
    ribbon, white or cream*
*3 small pots of fabric paint, 1 red, 1 blue,
    1 yellow; 3 small sponges*
*56 × 68cm (22 × 27 in) piece of 50g (2 oz)
    polyester wadding*
56 × 68cm (22 × 27 in) piece of lining fabric
*20 × 70cm (8 × 28 in) piece of fabric for bias-
    cut binding*
Matching sewing threads

Preparation

1   Colour the warp ribbons. Cut them to
64.5 cm (25 in) lengths. Mix each of the
fabric paints with a little water in three
saucers.
2   Sponge the colours onto the ribbons,
leaving some white spaces, following the
techniques described on page 12.
3   Leave to dry while you colour the lining
fabric and the binding fabric. Colour the
wider ribbon also.
4   Draw a 53 × 62cm (21 × 25 in) rectangle
on the adhesive side of the interfacing.

Weaving

5 Beginning and ending with a strip of the wide ribbon, pin the coloured warp ribbons down the marked-out coverlet pattern.

6 Cut the remaining 25mm (1 in)-wide ribbons for the weft (adding 2.5cm (1 in) to each length for seam allowance). Weave in an under 1, over 2 pattern.

7 Bond the finished weaving to the interfacing (page 16). The final pressing will also fix the fabric paints.

8 Prepare the weaving for quilting. Quilt diagonally (see picture) using either machine-stitching or by hand using running stitches.

9 Cut bias strips from the coloured fabric and bind the edges of the coverlet.

Other ideas

As modern polyester ribbons are machine-washable, other items can be made in ribbon weaving for a new baby. A useful changing pad could be made in similar dimensions to the coverlet but line it with a soft white towelling fabric. The pad could have ribbon ties stitched to the short ends so that it can be neatly rolled for travelling.

A base pad could be made for the bottom of a dressing basket, quilted in the same pattern as the jacket. Matching ribbons could be tied in bows to the basket handles. Bags and purses for cotton wool, tissues etc could be made from ribbon weaving and a small booklet for safety pins might have a ribbon-woven cover.

Quilting ribbon weaving

Quilting gives body to ribbon-woven fabric and, for garments and coverlets, adds warmth and softness. It also gives a decorative finish which enhances the weaving pattern.

Wadded quilting, the oldest technique, holds the top fabric (or weaving), a filling and the backing or lining together with stitches. Stitching can be worked with a sewing machine or, for traditionalists, can be worked by hand using running stitches. The quilting can be worked in lines following the lines of weaving, diagonally across the ribbons or in a random pattern.

The filling most used today is polyester wadding (do not use the wadding which has a 'skin' on it as this is not soft enough for the purpose). Wadding of 50g (2 oz) weight is used for quilting the baby jacket and coverlet on page 35 but a heavier wadding, 100g (4 oz) weight is usually used for larger coverlets or heavy garments where extra thickness is desired.

Carded sheep's wool can also be used for quilting.

Preparation

1 Cut the backing fabric and wadding to the same size as the weaving (or top fabric).

2 Spread the lining fabric wrong side up. Lay the wadding on top. Spread the weaving on the wadding, right side up.

3 Pin the 3 layers together, inserting a line of pins vertically, working from the middle, and then horizontally, smoothing the weaving as you pin. Pin round the edges also.

4 Thread a needle with a long length of basting thread. Work basting stitches in a 'grid' pattern, vertically and horizontally.

Remove the pins as you work, but keeping the surface of the work smooth

Quilting

5 Work quilting stitches through all layers using a sewing machine or by hand using running stitches. If you are using a sewing machine, roll the work under the machine's arm while stitching and reduce the presser foot tension so that the quilting passes under the machine's foot more easily.

Quilting without wadding

In some projects in this book, quilting is recommended to give backed weaving extra body, but a polyester wadding filling is not required.

Quilting with ribbons

Very narrow ribbons, 1.5mm (1/16 in)-wide, can be used for working running stitches if desired. Ends could be tied in bows at intersections to add texture to the weaving.

Velvet Cushion

The ribbons used to make the cushion pictured came from many different sources, some are old, some new. It is worth looking through your ribbon collection to see what you already have, and then building a colour scheme around them. Remember that not all old ribbons are colourfast and you may experience some colour-bleeding when bonding the weaving to the interfacing. Test ribbons by steam-pressing them on a piece of white fabric first.

Materials required
For a cushion 38 cm (15 in) square:
45cm (18 in) square of soft iron-on interfacing
4.80m (5¼ yd) of 15mm (⅝ in)-wide black velvet ribbon
2.40m (2⅝ yd) of 12mm (½ in)-wide black grosgrain ribbon
1.60m (1¾ yd) of 9mm (⅜ in)-wide royal blue satin ribbon
2.40m (2⅝ yd) of 15mm (⅝ in)-wide brown velvet ribbon
2.40m (2⅝ yd) of 6mm (¼ in)-wide brown grosgrain ribbon
3.25m (3½ yd) of 6mm (¼ in)-wide crimson velvet ribbon
2.40m (2⅝ yd) of 12mm (½ in)-wide navy satin ribbon
1.60m (1¾ yd) of 6mm (¼ in)-wide rust velvet ribbon
2.40m (2⅝ yd) of 1.5mm (1/16 in)-wide purple satin ribbon
3.25m (3½ yd) of 1.5mm (1/16 in)-wide cherry or coral satin ribbon
3.25m (3½ yd) of 1.5mm (1/16 in)-wide wine satin ribbon
3.25m (3½ yd) of 6mm (¼ in)-wide black velvet ribbon
2.40m (2⅝ yd) of black velvet tubular ribbon

43cm (17 in) square of fabric for backing
Feather cushion pad 38cm (15 in) square

Preparation
1   Draw a 43cm (17 in) square on the adhesive side of the interfacing. Pin the interfacing to a cork mat.
2   Cut all the ribbons (except the velvet tubing) into 40cm (16 in) lengths. Divide the ribbons into 2 equal piles, one pile for the warp, the other for the weft.

Weaving
3   Referring to the picture for colour sequence, pin the warp ribbons edge to edge along the top of the interfacing square.
4   Weave the weft ribbons in the same colour sequence, working an under 1, over 1 pattern. Pin the ribbons down at both ends.
5   Bond the ribbons to the interfacing (see page 16 for the technique). Remove the pins.
6   On the wrong side of the weaving, round off the corners of the marked square.

Making the cushion
7   Place the weaving and the velvet backing together right sides facing. Pin and baste 6mm (¼ in) outside the marked line.
8   Machine-stitch on the line starting about 5cm (2 in) from a corner, working round the corner, along 3 sides and then round the 4th corner, leaving a gap in the last seam for inserting the cushion pad.
9   Trim the seam allowance and turn the cushion cover to the right side. Press the seams lightly if necessary. Insert the cushion pad and slip-stitch the open seam.
10   Cut the velvet tubing in 4 pieces. Fold each piece and sew at the middle to the 4 corners. Oversew the tubing ends.

Ribbon weaving in furnishings

Ribbon weaving makes a strong, hard-wearing fabric and, as such, is taken seriously for upholstery by interior decorators. The weaving process enables special colour schemes to be formulated and this enhances its desirability.

In the home, ribbon-woven fabric can be used for re-covering chair seats and backs, stool tops, window cushions and bench covers. Outdoors, it can be used for swings, recovering hammocks, cushions, garden chair backs and seats, for new deck chair covers and for making covers for long cushions for recliner chairs.

For maximum strength, hard-wearing ribbons such as polyester grosgrain should be used and weaving can be combined with strips of fabric such as ticking and canvas.

It is important that both ribbons and fabrics be colourfast, washable or dry-cleanable so that the weaving will stand up to a lot of wear, exposure to strong light and, possibly, damp.

There are various ways of making the finished weaving even stronger. The method used for making the garden cushions on pages 42-43, for instance, where ribbons have been stitched to strong fabric before weaving, is one option. Ribbons can also be over-stitched before weaving, or the finished fabric can be quilted.

Re-covering a chair seat

Preparation
Remove the old seat cover carefully and use it to make a paper pattern. Spread the old fabric on a sheet of paper and draw round the outline.

Use the pattern to draw the weaving area on the adhesive side of medium-weight iron-on interfacing. Pin the interfacing to a cork mat or, if the area is large, to a thickly padded table top.

Weave the ribbons (and fabric strips) in the pattern of your choice, perhaps choosing one from pages 20-21, 22-23 and bond the weaving to the interfacing (refer to page 16).

Mounting the weaving
Strengthen the weaving by backing it with a piece of strong calico. To do this, spread the weaving, right side up, on the fabric and pin and baste horizontally and vertically and then round the edges. Machine-stitch the weaving to the backing fabric, stitching between the ribbons through all thicknesses. Then work two or three rows of stitching round the outside edge. Trim the weaving to shape if necessary using the paper pattern.

Dampen the weaving with cold, clear water (this will help make the woven fabric easier to handle). Lay the damp fabric on the chair seat and, using a staple gun or upholster's tacks, fasten the fabric to the chair frame. Begin at the middle of the sides, then work towards the corners, stretching the fabric smoothly. To finish, glue braid over the raw edges of the fabric.

If you prefer, make a flat braid of toning ribbons (page 81) and use this instead of bought braid. Turn the braid (or plait) ends under and butt the ends, oversewing a neat join to finish.

Weaving patterns chosen for furnishings should be practical. Choose a closely woven texture rather than one which has long 'overs' and 'unders' in the weave, as the ribbons tend to catch in use. A three-layer pattern, such as the weave Fig 10 on page 22.

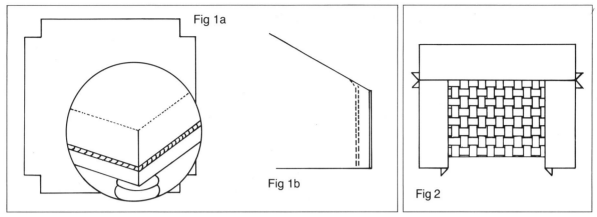

Fig 1a The template shape for overstuffed seat; Fig 1b the corner seam double-stitched; the stitched corner fitted to the seat

Fig 2 Woven insert: machine stitch the side strips over the weaving, press back, then machine-stitch the top strip over the side strips

Overstuffed furniture

If the chair seat or stool top is overstuffed, you will need to make a template pattern similar to Fig 1a. When the weaving has been completed and backed, machine-stitch the corner seams, tapering and curving the end of the seam so that the cover fits the chair seat tightly (Fig 1b). When working the seam, two rows of machine-stitching will be stronger than one. Fit the corners on the furniture.

Re-covering a deck chair

For a deck chair, where you will be working with a long length of weaving, it is advisable to work on a large table padded with a folded blanket, or perhaps on a blanket on the floor. Make up the weaving using either the interfacing method or the fabric-backing method (page 16). If you decide upon the interfacing method, back the weaving with either mattress ticking or canvas.

Machine-stitch through the weaving and backing, stitching in both directions along the ribbon edges, at 8cm (3¼ in) intervals.

Bind the long edges with 5cm (2 in)-wide grosgrain ribbon, working 2 rows of machine stitching. Cut lengths of the same ribbon for the top and bottom ends of the cover. Machine-stitch, one edge to the cover.

Fold these ribbon strips over the top and bottom rails and pin.

Using a long, sharp, strong needle and button thread, sew the cover to the chair using back-stitch.

If you wish to quilt the deck chair cover, do this after finishing the weaving. Spread the backing fabric wrong side up. Lay polyester wadding on the fabric and then spread the weaving on top, right side up. Pin the three layers together and work basting stitches, vertically and horizonally and then along the edges. Machine-stitch through all layers, using normal tension and a medium stitch length, stitching between the lines of ribbons. (You will have to roll the cover under the arm of the machine to stitch it).

Bind the edges of the cover as described, and attach to the frame in the same way.

Woven inserts

Ribbon weaving looks very effective when it is set into a 'frame' of fabric.

Make a paper pattern of the stool top or seat to be worked. Decide the area to be woven. Draw this area on a piece of interfacing and complete the weaving and bonding. For the frame, cut strips of fabric to the depth and width of the frame plus 12mm (½ in) on both measurements. Cut 2 side strips and 2 horizontal strips. Machine-stitch the side strips to the edges of the weaving, right sides together and press back the strips. Lay the horizontal strips on the weaving, right sides facing and machine-stitch (Fig 2). Press back.

Garden cushions

In this project, strips of fabric are applied to ribbons and then woven. The resulting fabric is very tough and hard-wearing and can be used to make sturdy furnishings, such as the two garden cushions pictured. The colour schemes are planned to complement outdoor surroundings, a garden, the patio or even a garden room, but alternative colours can, of course, be substituted. Mattress ticking is used for the strips and for the cushion backs.

Large shopping bags or shoulder bags could also be made with the weaving technique. A good size would be $52 \times 42 \times 20$cm ($21 \times 16\frac{1}{2} \times 8$ in).

Materials required
For cushions 38cm (15 in) square:
Green cushion:
4 fabric strips 6 × 42cm (2¼ × 16½ in), A
8 fabric strips 3.5 × 42cm (1¼ ×16½ in), B
16 fabric strips 1.5 × 42cm (⅝ × 16½ in), C
Ribbons as follows:
5.25m (5¾ yd) of 6mm (¼ in)-wide satin in light moss green (a); 6.85m (7½ yd) of 6mm (¼ in)-wide satin in dark moss green (b); 2.75m (3 yd) of 9mm (⅜ in)-wide dark green velvet (c); 1.85m (2 yd) of 6mm (¼ in)-wide grey velvet (d).
Grey and white cushion:
4 fabric strips 5 × 42cm (2 × 16½ in)
4 fabric strips 4 × 42cm (1½ × 16½ in)
4 fabric strips 3 × 42cm (1¼ × 16½ in)
16 fabric strips 1.5 × 42cm (⅝ × 16½ in)
Ribbons as follows:
3.25m (3.5 yd) × 1.5mm (1/16 in)-wide
3.25m (3.5 yd) of 10mm (⅜ in)-wide
5.10m (5.5 yd) of 6mm (¼ in)-wide
Sewing threads to match ribbons
42cm (16½ in) square of mattress ticking to back both cushions

Preparation
1   For the green cushion, fold the long edges of the fabric strips to the wrong side, overlapping the edges slightly, and press the folds.
2   Using a medium-width zigzag stitch, apply ribbons to the strips as follows:
    A strips, b and c ribbons
    B1 strips, a and b ribbons (work 4 strips)
    B2 strips, b and c ribbons (work 4 strips)
    C1 strips, a ribbons (work 8 strips)
    C2 strips, b ribbons (work 4 strips)
    C3 strips, d ribbons (work 4 strips)
    Follow the picture for positioning ribbons on the fabric strips.
3   Work the grey and white cushion strips as shown in the picture.
4   Draw a 42cm (16½ in) square on kitchen paper or dressmaker's squared paper. Pin the paper to a cork mat.

Weaving
5   For the green cushion, pin one of the A ribbons to the top right edge. Pin the other ribbons, edges touching, as follows:
B2, C2, B1, C3, C1, C1, C1, C1, C3, B1, C2, B2, A.
    Pin the bottom edges.
6   Using a plain weave, weave the weft ribbons in the same order.
7   Pin down both ends of the weft ribbons then pin the ribbons to each other all round the edges of the weaving, removing the securing pins. Lift the weaving from the cork mat.
8   Baste the edges of the weaving, removing the pins. Machine-stitch close to the edge.
9   Make up the cushion, following the technique described on page 104. Work the grey and white cushion from the picture.

Ecclesiastical work

As ribbon weaving can produce a richly coloured and textured fabric, it is ideal for making and decorating church furnishings and vestments, such as the burse.

Other things which can be made include the altar frontal, the pulpit fall, kneelers and alms bags. In vestments, the chasuble, cope, mitre and stole could all have some areas of ribbon weaving as decoration.

Ways of using ribbon weaving

For larger areas of fabric, such as the altar frontal, a deep woven ribbon border can be applied. This is an opportunity for dramatic impact and metallic ribbons are ideal in this context, perhaps mixed with velvet and satin ribbons. The weaving pattern could be denser at the hem edge and develop into spaced weaving higher up. Ribbons can be overstitched with metallic threads to catch the light and the entire piece could be quilted, working between the ribbons both vertically and horizontally.

Simple motifs can be made up in ribbon weaving – squares, rectangles, diamonds etc – and decorated with machine embroidery.

Ribbon weaving can, of course, be used to construct an entire item and beautiful colour schemes are possible with a simple over 1, under 1 weave. Three-dimensional effects can be achieved, using the juxtaposition of light and dark ribbons to give a gradual change of tone and focus the eye.

Weaving and appliqué

More complex shapes for motifs can be worked in appliqué and then attached with sewing to a ribbon woven background. Surface embroidery can be added for further embellishment. Pictorial motifs – doves, fish etc – are popular in ecclesiastical work but more abstract designs are beginning to be accepted by both clergy and congregations.

Ribbons through fabric

The various techniques described in Chapter Five, needleweaving ribbon through even-weave fabrics, and through drawn threads, can be used to decorate fabrics for church furnishings and vestments. Linen, for instance, with its creamy, matt texture, contrasts superbly with the lustre of satin ribbons. Ribbons can be woven in massed bands on altar frontals, pulpit falls, stoles etc, or they can be worked in linear designs across the piece.

Ribbons through canvas

Ribbons woven through canvas is a suitable technique to use for making articles such as kneelers, bench and seat cushions, burses and for book covers. Canvas is itself hard wearing and when woven with polyester ribbons, a beautiful surface is produced which will resist any amount of hard wear and exposure. Polyester ribbons withstand light and are unlikely to fade over the years and will stand up to damp conditions which prevail in many churches.

Colour schemes

The initial design, worked out in colour on paper, should of course be discussed with the vicar or priest and considered in the correct setting. It is possible that the liturgical colours will be required as follows:
White or *gold* for Saints' Days, weddings and feast days. *Red* for Whitsun, the third Sunday in Advent and for some feast days. *Blue* or *violet* for Lent and Advent. *Green* for the

season of Trinity to Advent, and some feast days. *Rose pink* can be used after Trinity. *Purple* (mainly in the Roman Church) for Advent and part of Lent. *Off-white* is often used for Lent.

Making a burse

A burse is the folder which holds the folded chalice veil between services and stands, open, on the altar during the service.

Materials required

Finished size: 23cm (9 in) square
25.5cm (10¼ in) square of single thread
  canvas, 10 threads to 2.5cm (1 in)
2 balls of bronze-coloured tubular knitting
  ribbon
1 ball of dull silver-coloured tubular knitting
  ribbon
1 ball of shiny bronze-coloured knitting yarn
10m (11 yd) of bronze-coloured satin ribbon
2 pieces of stiff card 23cm (9 in) square
2 pieces of stiff card 20cm (8 in) square
Rust-coloured velvet fabric, white linen fabric
Strong thread, quick-drying adhesive
Matching sewing threads

Preparation

1 Mark a 23cm (9 in) square on the canvas using a waterproof felt-tipped pen. Draw in the cross (refer to the picture on page 47).

Working the embroidery

2 Using the bronze and dull silver-coloured tubular knitting ribbons, work the cross in Florentine stitch over 2, 3 and 4 threads, referring to the picture of the burse for the pattern. Add highlights in the shiny knitting yarn.

3 Lay bronze knitting ribbon over the whole area from top to bottom, going through to the back of the canvas behind the cross.

4 Cut a length of satin ribbon and turn the end to the wrong side. Sew the end to the edge of the cross and weave horizontally through the bronze knitting ribbon warp. Stay-stitch to secure.

Finishing

5 Place one of the larger card pieces on the wrong side of the worked canvas and turn the edges onto the card. Insert pins at the edges to hold the canvas while you lace the canvas edges (Fig 2). Cover the second piece of card in the same way with velvet. Cover the two smaller pieces of card with white linen, using the same lacing technique.

6 Glue the linen-covered card pieces to the backs of the front burse pieces. Leave to dry.

7 Make a hinge of velvet and sew between the front and back pieces.

8 Work a buttonhole-stitched bar between the burse front and back so that it stands up.

Fig 1   Mark a cross on the canvas as shown

Fig 2   Pin the canvas to the card, inserting pins into the card edges. Lace with strong thread vertically and then horizontally

Fig 3   Work a buttonhole-stitched bar between the front and back so that the burse stands up

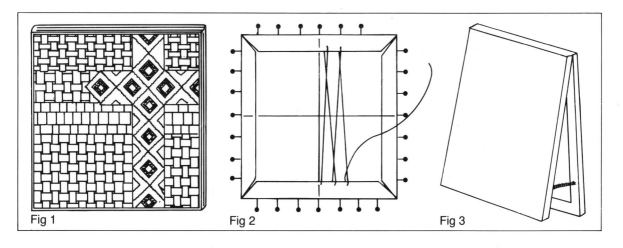

Fig 1   Fig 2   Fig 3

Ribbon-woven file

Ribbon-woven file and book covers make wonderful gifts and can be made to mark special occasions, such as weddings, anniversaries or birthdays.

Materials required

1 looseleaf file 23 × 24 × 3cm (9 × 9½ × 1¼ in)

2.30m (2½ yd) of 35mm (1¼ in)-wide hounds-tooth check ribbon in dark blue and black, A

75cm (30 in) of 25mm (1 in)-wide satin ribbon in royal blue, B

50cm (20 in) 12mm (½ in)-wide satin ribbon in royal blue, C

3m (3¾ yd) 25mm (1 in)-wide moiré ribbon in black, D

2.40m (2⅝ yd) of 15mm (⅝ in)-wide velvet ribbon in black, E

1.40m (1½ yd) of 15mm (⅝ in)-wide velvet ribbon in navy blue, F

1m (1⅛ yd) 15mm (⅝ in)-wide gold ribbon, black edged, G

2.30m (2½ yd) of 9mm (⅜ in)-wide gold ribbon, black edged, H

1.50m (1⅝ yd) of 3mm (⅛ in)-wide gold ribbon, black edged, I

1m (1⅛ yd) of 1.5mm (1/16 in)-wide gold ribbon, black edged, J

70 × 45cm (28 × 18 in) piece of calico

1 rectangular embroidery frame (or old picture frame) with inside measurement of 60 × 36cm (24 × 14 in)

50 × 28cm (20 × 11 in) piece of lining fabric to tone with the ribbons

2 pieces of card 21.5 × 23cm (8½ × 9 in)

Preparation

1   Mount the calico on the frame with drawing pins, keeping the grain of the fabric parallel with the edges. Make sure that the fabric is taut in both directions.

2   Mark a rectangle on the calico measuring 58 × 32cm (23 × 13 in)

3   Cut and lay the horizontal ribbons as follows: A, E, F, D, A, D, E, B, A, D, A Pin the ribbon ends to the calico.

4   Cut and lay the first diagonal ribbons slanting from the top left to bottom right, (ribbons F, E, F, D, D, E, F, D, F, C, B, C) leaving spaces between them. The spaces can be regular or irregular. Pin the ribbon ends to the calico keeping all the ribbons parallel.

5   Cut the gold ribbons (ribbons G, H and I) for the third layer and weave them under the horizontal ribbons and over the diagonal ones as follows: J, H, I, H, G, G, H, J, I, I, H, H, J, H. The spaces can be regular or irregular, and sometimes an 'under' or 'over' can be missed out.

6   Because this is not a tight weave, the ribbons must then be machine-stitched to the calico to secure them, using toning sewing thread. Work stitches along both edges of all ribbons.

7   Remove the fabric from the frame, and lay it face down on a table.

8   Open the file and lay it on the calico. Fold the fabric at the top and bottom of the spine onto the file, turn a hem and glue the hem down, pulling the fabric taut from top to bottom. Allow to dry under pressure. Note that the file's spine only is worked at this stage.

9   Fold the front and back edges of the fabric to the inside of the file (hold the file ▶

Right: The burse instructions are on page 45.
Instructions for making the blue and black file cover continue onto page 48

closed as you do this), and hold temporarily with clips. Pin then fold mitres on all four corners, sewing them neatly. Turn a hem on the front and back edges and glue the hems down. Allow to dry under pressure.

10   Turn a hem on the top and bottom edges (back and front). Thread a needle with strong thread and lace the hems from top to bottom. (These hems can be glued if you prefer but lacing is more efficient.)

11   Cut the lining fabric in half. Lay a piece of card on each piece centring it. Fold the fabric over the edges of the cards and glue them, mitring the corners. When dry, glue one piece to the inside of the front cover, and one to the back. Dry under pressure.

Wedding bible

A family bible represents generations of love. For the special day, weave ribbons into a luxurious cover for it and sew a ribbon rose and streamers to the front.

Materials required

For a 13.7 × 20cm (5½ × 8 in) bible:
45cm (18 in) iron-on interfacing
7.50m (8¼ yd) single-faced satin ribbon, 22mm (⅞ in)-wide

Preparation

1   Cut a rectangle of interfacing 23 × 56cm (9 × 22 in). Draw a shape 16 × 50cm (6½ × 20 in).

2   Pin to a cork mat adhesive side up.

3   Cut the warp ribbons 2.5cm (1 in) deeper than the drawn rectangle.

Weaving

4   Pin the warp ribbons along the top edge of the drawn rectangle, overlapping the edge by about 12mm (½ in) and edges touching.

5   Cut the weft ribbons 2.5cm (1 in) longer than the drawn rectangle. Weave through the warp in an under 1, over 1 weave, pinning the ribbons down at both ends.

6   Bond the ribbons to the interfacing (refer to page 16). Remove the pins.

7   Machine-stitch all round the weaving just outside the drawn line and trim the ribbon ends.

8   Right sides together, fold the ends back 5cm (2 in) and pin. Try the cover on the bible to check the fit when the bible is closed.

9   Baste and machine-stitch along the folded ends, taking 6mm (¼ in) seams (Fig 1).

10   Trim the corners diagonally and turn to the right side.

11   Turn the top and bottom edges to the wrong side and glue down.

12   Insert the bible in the cover. Roses made from ribbons can be sewn to the cover. (See illustration).

Markers

If a ribbon bookmark is required, weave two or three 3mm (⅛ in)-wide ribbons, or a single length of 2.5cm (1 in)-wide ribbon, into the warp at the position where the bible spine will be (see Fig 2).

Fig 1   Fold the ends 5cm (2 in) to the wrong side and machine-stitch at top and bottom

Fig 2   Ribbon bookmarks can be woven in while weaving the bible cover

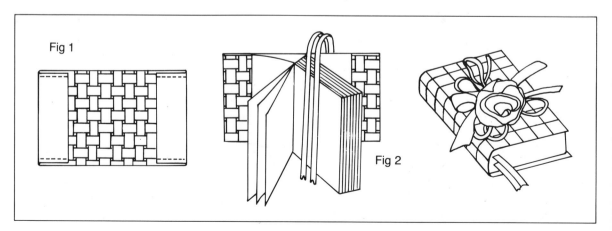

Fig 1

Fig 2

Breakfast set

The ribbons for the place mat and egg cosy were marbled (refer to page 13 for the technique), but any printed or woven ribbons could be used instead. Choose colours to match your china and which will look bright and appealing in the morning. Several of the weaving patterns on pages 20-21, 22-23 can be worked instead of the over 1, under 1 weave recommended here. Narrow ribbons are used to make the egg cosy as this is a smaller item.

Place mat

Dimensions: 38 × 25cm (15 × 10 in)
38 × 25cm (15 × 10 in) piece of card
45 × 30cm (18 × 12 in) piece of iron-on inter-
*   facing*
2.50m (2¾ yd) of 38mm (1½ in)-wide satin
*   ribbon*
1.40m (1½ yd) of 6mm (¼ in)-wide ribbon
2.30m (2½ yd) of 3mm (⅛ in)-wide ribbon
1.50m (1 ⅝ yd) of satin bias binding
Matching sewing threads
38 × 25cm (15 × 10 in) piece of felt

Preparation

1   Marble the 38mm (1½ in)-wide ribbon, referring to page 13 for the technique.
2   Round off the corners of the piece of card, using an eggcup as a guide. Cut out the shape to use as a template.
3   Place the template on the adhesive side of the interfacing and draw round it. Pin the interfacing to a cork mat.
4   Cut the marbled ribbon into 10 pieces each 25cm (10 in) long.

Weaving

5   Pin the marbled ribbons along the top edge of the drawn rectangle, edges touching.

6   Cut the 6mm (¼ in)-wide ribbons 38cm (15 in) long and weave in an under 1, over 1 weave, setting ribbons approximately 2.5cm (1 in) apart (see picture). Pin at both ends.
7   Cut the 3mm (⅛ in)-wide ribbons and weave them diagonally over and under the marbled ribbons as shown.
8   Bond the ribbons to the interfacing and remove the pins. Pin the ends of the narrow ribbons to the wide ribbons to keep them in place.
9   Place the card template on the weaving and draw round it with chalk or a water-proof pen.

Place the woven fabric, right side up, on the felt and pin together at the edges. Machine-stitch on the marked line.
10   Trim the mat 4mm (³⁄₁₆ in) outside the stitching line.   ▶

Fig 1   Graph pattern for the egg cosy, scale 1 sq = 2.5cm (1 in). The breakfast set picture is on page 51

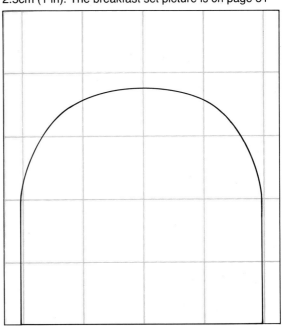

11 Quilt the mat by stitching between the wide ribbons working in alternate directions (this avoids distorting the weaving). The stitching should catch in the narrow ribbons.

12 Bind the edges of the mat.

Egg cosy

Materials required

For one cosy:

Squared dressmaker's paper, scale 1 sq = 2.5cm (1 in)

15 × 30cm (6× 12 in)-piece of soft iron-on interfacing

15 × 30cm (6 × 12 in) piece of felt

1.50m (1⅝ yd) of 25mm (1 in)-wide ribbon

8.40 (9¼ yd) of 3mm (⅛ in)-wide satin ribbon

75cm (30 in) of satin bias binding

Matching threads

Preparation

1 Marble the 25mm (1 in)-wide ribbon as instructed on page 13.

2 Draw the shape from Fig 1 on squared paper, scale 1 sq = 2.5cm (1 in). Trace down onto thin card to make a template. Cut out.

3 Lay the template on the adhesive side of the interfacing. Draw round it, then move the template and draw round it again to make a front and back for the cosy.

4 Pin the interfacing to a cork mat.

Weaving

Cut the 25mm (1 in)-wide ribbons in 10 15cm (6 in) pieces and pin to the interfacing along the straight bottom edges of both shapes, edges touching.

5 Cut the narrow ribbons into 15cm (6 in) lengths and weave into the wide ribbons in an over 1, under 1 weave, pinning the ends (see picture).

6 Bond the ribbons to the interfacing and remove the pins.

7 Use the card template to mark the outline of the front and back egg cosy pieces on the weaving. Cut out the shapes about 25mm (1 in) from the marked line.

8 Machine-stitch on the line. Trim both pieces 4mm (³/₁₆ in) from the stitched line.

9 Quilt the pieces, machine-stitching between the wider ribbons.

10 Bind the bottom, straight edges with bias binding. Pin and baste the front and back together and then bind all round.

Napkin Ring

A napkin ring, similar to the one in the picture opposite, can be made by weaving ribbons over a wooden or plastic ring.

Alternatively, make a ring from cardboard tubing. Cut three 5cm (2 in) 'slices' from a 4cm (1⅝ in) diameter tube. Cut 2 pieces open and glue them round the third piece to make a stronger cardboard ring (Fig 2). Wind narrow ribbon over the ring to completely cover it, making an odd number of winds (Fig 3). Glue the ends on the inside. Weave ribbons through the warp (see picture). You may find that a curved upholstery needle is useful for weaving narrow ribbons when working on small items with curved surfaces.

Fig 2 Cut through the pieces of tube, then glue pieces around the tube to make a strong cardboard ring

Fig 3 To make the warp, wind 9mm (³/₈ in)-wide ribbon round the ring to cover it, edges touching and making an odd number of winds

Right: Breakfast set in ribbon weaving, with a hot-water bottle cover worked with ribbons through fabric (page 78) ▶

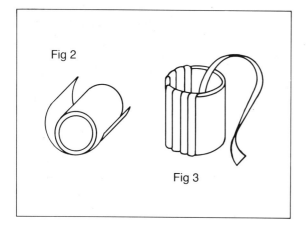

Fig 2

Fig 3

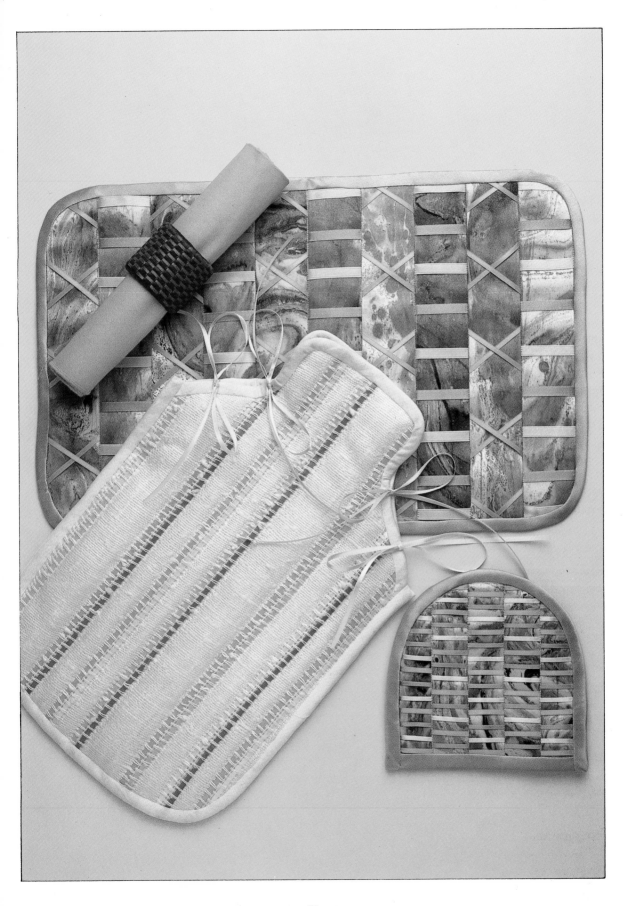

Ribbon neckties

Ribbon-woven ties can be worn by both men and women, although different colour schemes for each might be chosen. Quantities for weaving a 'kipper'-shaped tie (see illustration) with 12mm (½ in)-wide ribbons are given but if the pattern is adapted or different ribbons are used the ribbon quantities will also need to be adapted. For instance, if 6mm (¼ in)-wide ribbon is being used, the quantity is doubled. If 3mm (⅛ in)-wide ribbon is used, four times the length is needed. If you decide on a combination of widths, approximately three to four times the quantity given will be required. The necktie is worked in a plain weave but some of the weaves illustrated on pages 20-21, 22-23 can be used. Velvet or grosgrain ribbons are not recommended for weaving ties as they are too bulky.

Kipper tie

Materials required

Dressmaker's squared paper scale 1 sq = 2.5cm (1 in)
65 × 75cm (25½ × 30 in) piece of silk or cotton fabric
65 × 75cm (25½ × 30 in) piece of lining fabric
26 × 46cm (10¼ × 18 in) piece of thin card
4m (4⅜ yd) each of 12mm (½ in)-wide single faced satin (or taffeta) ribbon in four colours
26 × 51cm (10¼ × 20 in) piece of iron-on interfacing
Matching sewing threads

Preparation

1   Draw the graph pattern (Fig 1) onto dressmaker's squared paper (scale 1 sq = 2.5cm (1 in). A seam allowance of 6mm (¼ in) is included. (An old tie can be used as a pattern if you prefer.) Cut out the 2 pattern pieces, and pencil in all pattern markings.

2   Make a card template of the Aa section (on pattern A) marked by the broken line.

3   Place the template on the adhesive side of the interfacing pinned to a cork mat or pin board. Draw round the shape and mark in the arrow and the x-points (Fig 1).

4   Pin the paper pattern AaA on the right side of the tie fabric, matching the grain to the directional arrow. Cut out the shape. Pin the pattern B to the tie fabric, matching the grain to the directional arrow.

Cut out the shape. Cut the lining, using pattern pieces AaA and B.

Weaving

5   Following the directional arrow on Aa, cut the warp ribbons to fit the interfacing shape and pin them down at both ends.

6   Cut the weft ribbons to fit the shape, weave them through the warp ribbons at right angles, in a plain weave, pinning down at both ends.

7   Bond the finished weaving to the interfacing. Trim ribbon edges to the pattern line.

8   Lay the ribbon weaving right side up on the right side of fabric piece AaA, matching edges, and pin. Stay-stitch all round, stitching close to the edges.

9   Machine-stitch the weaving to the fabric, working between the lines of ribbon in both directions, and taking care not to stretch the bias edges. (Stitching removes the need for an interlining and prevents the weaving moving about in wear.)

10   Stitch piece B to AaA, right sides together, matching C-D, E-F. Stitch 6mm

(¼ in) from the edge. Press the seam open.

11　Join lining pieces AaA and B in the same way but leaving C-D, E-F open. Press the seams open.

12　Lay the lining on the tie, wrong sides together. Machine-stitch round the wide end from x through x to x. Stitch 6mm (¼ in) from the edge. Clip into the seam allowance at x on both edges of the tie. Stitch the narrow end of the tie in the same way from x through x to x. Clip into the seam allowance at x.

13　Baste the seams on the right side all round the tie to hold the seam flat, pulling out the stitched seam with a pin.

14　Machine-stitch 6mm (¼ in) from the edges all round the tie. Turn the tie to the right side through C-D, E-F and press, taking care not to press the seams. (The best way to do this is to push a padded broom handle into the tie and press over that).

15　Remove basting threads and then press the seams again. Close the open seam with slip stitches.

Straight Tie

Ties are usually made on the bias of fabric so that they knot easily without wrinkles.

Fig 1　Graph pattern for the 'kipper' tie, scale 1 sq = 2.5cm (1 in)

However, a tie can be made on the straight grain, which uses less fabric and ribbon.

This type is generally worn by women, loosely knotted round the neck so that it does not look too masculine. Good colour schemes might be gold, mid-blue and rust, or pale yellow, pale blue and pink, or rust, blue and grey. For evening, black, gold and copper or white, grey and silver would look dramatic.

The instructions here are for a straight tie 5cm (2 in) wide by 126cm (50 in) long. Narrow ribbons, 6mm, 9mm or 12mm (¼ in, ⅜ in or ½ in)-wide could be used.

1　Draw an outline on the adhesive-side of iron-on interfacing 35 × 6cm (14 × 2½ in). Seam allowance is included. Weave ribbons on the straight-grain, using the weave pattern of your choice (pages 20-21, 22-23).

2　Cut a piece of matching fabric 15 × 6cm (6 × 2½ in) and stitch to the end of the weaving, right sides facing.

3　Cut a piece of lining fabric to the overall dimensions. Pin and baste to the weaving piece, right sides facing. Machine-stitch all round, leaving a 5cm (2 in) gap in one long side.

4　Turn the tie right side out. Pull out the corners and the seam edges with a pin. Baste the edges. Press.

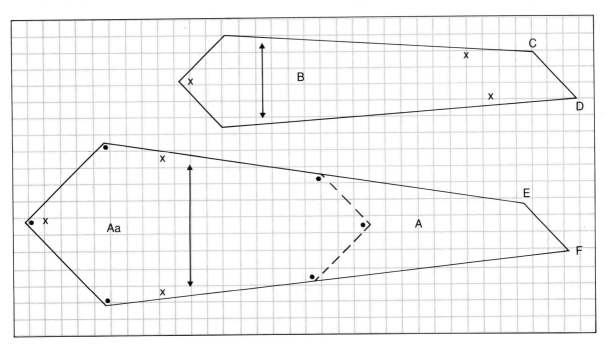

CHAPTER FOUR

Weaving through fabric

Ribbons woven through fabric gives quite a different look to ribbon weaving, and the ribbon becomes part of the fabric. If ribbon is woven through a soft net or mesh, the result is very soft and pliable and is suitable for scarves, shawls and jackets. The Fishing net jacket on page 57 is an example.

Woven through stiff canvas, the ribbon weaving is more suitable for making items such as belts and bags (see the Saddlebag on page 72), or for making set-in or applied details on medium or heavy-weight fabric garments – pocket flaps, collars, yokes or shoulder epaulettes.

This type of ribbon weaving is, in effect, a needleweaving technique and although the ribbons can be worked vertically, horizontally or diagonally, the base fabric is not totally covered with ribbon, but this effect is possible also if that is what you want.

The base fabric can be dyed, painted or sprayed to change the original colour or to decorate the fabric, and the dye or paint used must be correct for the fibre content of the fabric. (Refer to the section on dyeing and painting in Chapter One, pages 10-15).

Car spray is very useful for colouring small areas, and this comes in a wide range of shades including gold and silver and metallic finishes. Do not use too much of this paint as it tends to stiffen the fabric. Car spray-painted fabrics can be washed and dry-cleaned.

Gold and silver spray paint used for Christmas decorations can also be used on canvas but this type, and car paint, should be used outdoors or next to an open window as the smell and fumes are rather unpleasant.

Ribbon weaving through a mesh fabric produces a soft, rather floppy fabric but if a firmer fabric is required for a garment or a bag perhaps, the woven mesh can be backed with wadding and then lining fabric, and afterwards quilted. This produces a soft, warm fabric and, if quilted closely enough, it can be laundered (as long as the ribbons are colourfast). ▶

Above: Painted ribbons woven through painted square-mesh net   *Betty Marsh*

Right: Layers of red felt stitched to green felt at intervals. The red felt was then cut away through alternate rows of stitching and slits cut in the remaining slits. Ribbon was woven through and twisted before being reinserted into the same fold

For other kinds of openweave fabrics suitable for weaving, look for gold and silver mesh fabrics which make glamorous shawls and scarves when woven with thin, delicate ribbons and tubular knitting ribbons. Fishing net is another alternative; the mesh is quite large, and the fabric is inexpensive and, woven with ribbons, might be an interesting idea for window curtains or room dividers.

There is scope also for experimental work using other unlikely fabrics, such as loose knitting or crochet made from metallic sewing threads.

Weaving through net

It is possible to make your own knotted filet net (see page 60) and a similarly suitable fabric can also be crocheted. Alternatively, loose, loopy knitting, worked in a fine thread, produces a mesh with hole of a different shape, which is very pliable and stretchy. Any of these hand-made fabrics would look superb worked in a gold or silver thread, or one that changes along its length.

Ribbon woven through net gives the fabric a beautiful handle and the result is, of course, reversible.

Although dress net is not really suitable for weaving through because the holes are too small, there are many other large mesh nets available with either square, hexagonal or diamond-shaped holes. Curtain nets, and millinery nets are all suitable.

Basic techniques

A large-eyed, blunt-tipped needle is used for ribbon needleweaving. You can use a ribbon that comfortably fills the holes, or two or three ribbons together or even mix ribbons and yarns. Soft ribbons, chosen too wide for the holes, will crush as they are woven and give a rich texture. Thin ribbon, or one that is smooth and shiny, may pull out of the net easily, and should be stitched to the net at the ends of rows or knotted to the net.

To work, spread the net flat on the table as this makes it easier to weave through and helps to keep the tension correct. It is very easy to pull the ribbons too tight and pucker the fabric. Leave the ribbons a little loose as you pull them through.

When weaving, ribbons can become twisted, which slows work down. Try holding the loop of ribbon with the left hand as you pull the needle through and this will help to keep it flat.

Experiment with effects by using ribbons stitched to ribbons, or printed, painted or dyed ribbons. Another idea to try might be a ribbon-woven net scarf in white on white, with a design paint sponged onto it afterwards.

Fishing net jacket

The fronts and back of the jacket pictured on page 59 are made from black fishing net with square, 2.5cm (1 in) holes, woven with a combination of satin ribbons, knitting ribbons and knitting and weaving yarns. The sleeves are made of black cotton fabric. Choose a commercial paper pattern similar in shape to Fig 1, without darts or curved edges. The jacket can be lined or left unlined.

The inspiration for the colour scheme for the ribbon weaving came from a rusty, corrugated iron shed seen in the county of Somerset in south-west England. It is amazing what beautiful colour schemes can evolve from unlikely sources, if one looks closely enough. Do not look at the object itself – just look at the colours.

If, when working a colour scheme, an exact match cannot be found in ribbon colours then mix ribbons with yarns, as in the jacket pictured.

Estimating ribbon quantities
The paper pattern will tell you how much net fabric you need. Estimating total ribbon quantities is more difficult. To obtain a rough estimate, measure the pattern pieces from shoulder to hem and decide how many lengths of ribbon will be woven through the net across a given width – 5cm (2 in) perhaps. By a simple calculation, you can assess roughly how much ribbon is required to work across all the jacket pieces.

Preparation
Lay the Jacket Front and Back pattern pieces under the net, matching the directional straight grain arrows with the vertical and horizontal threads. Cut an extra Front pattern piece from another piece of paper and lay this under the net, reversing it, so that you have 2 Fronts. Hold the pattern pieces to the net with pieces of sticky tape.

Cut out round the patterns roughly, leaving about 5cm (2 in) extra net all round the shape. Outline the patterns with sewing thread, taking the thread round the net threads so that the outline can be clearly seen. Work the weaving with the net still taped to the patterns.

Weaving
1   Lay the pieces of mounted net flat on a table. Using a long bodkin, weave the ribbons and yarns through the holes from top to bottom in an under 1, over 1 weave. Use 1, 2 or 3 lengths of ribbon together in the bodkin or one length of ribbon with 2 or 3

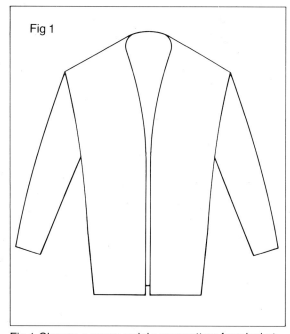

Fig 1 Choose a commercial paper pattern for a jacket similar to this shape, without darts or complicated details

yarns, or yarns only. Leave at least 1cm (⅜ in) hanging free at each end. Continue weaving down the net, until all the holes are filled. Work all the pieces in the same way. Remove the paper patterns.

2   Stay-stitch round the edges of all pieces to secure the ribbons. Stitch 2 rows. Cut the ribbon ends so that the correct shape of each piece is achieved.

3   Cut out and make up the Jacket Sleeves as described in the pattern instructions. Sew or machine-stitch the sleeves into the jacket.

4   If the jacket is to be left unlined, bind the raw edges of the weaving with bias-cut fabric strips to neaten them.

5   To line the jacket, use the pattern pieces to cut out 2 Fronts, 1 Back and 2 Sleeves from lining fabric. Make up the lining as described in the pattern instructions. Slip the lining onto the jacket, right sides facing. Machine-stitch all round, leaving a 25cm (10 in) gap in the Back hem. Turn right side out.

Finishing
6   Close the open seam with slip-stitches. Turn the sleeve hem and lining to the inside and slip-stitch together.

Ideas for fishing net
Because fishing net has a large mesh, it should be used for fairly large articles such as jackets and coats, cloaks and capes, curtains, blinds and door curtains. A bed-head could be covered with this type of weaving, the colours chosen to fit into the bedroom decor. A canopy might be made to match to simulate a four-poster bed.

Make a bed cover as a square so that one point lies on the pillow, one over the foot of the bed and a point hanging on each side. Knot the ribbon ends to make a natural fringe and no further finishing is required. This technique can also be used to make rugs, throws and shawls.

In the garden, a hammock of woven fishing net would be extremely comfortable, and strong, to lie upon. Quite bulky ribbons and yarns are required to weave through the mesh, but if 2 or 3 strands are used together, the holes are quickly filled.

A simple over 1, under 1, or over 2, under 2 weave looks attractive but for added texture, ribbons and yarns can be twisted, looped or knotted during the weaving process. For some projects, such as curtains and blinds, large wooden beads could be threaded on the ribbons, or curtain rings, which have been buttonhole-stitched to cover them. Ready-made cords can be added to the weaving, with small tassels tied on at random points. This would look particularly effective on a cloak, where the body's movement would make the tassels swing.

For experimental work, weaving need not be worked straight through the mesh, but could travel backwards and forwards, filling in some areas quite solidly, and leaving others empty. Areas of very fine weaving could contrast with areas of thick, textured weaving.

Fishing net is very tough and strong, and is usually washable, and colourfast. Choose polyester ribbons which are also washable and colourfast and there is no reason why the whole article cannot be washed. After spin drying, spread woven fishing net weaving to dry, flat if possible.

Right: The fishing net jacket back view, showing the deep, easy armhole which is an ideal shape for the fabric

Filet or fisherman's net

For centuries, fishermen, and embroiderers have made filet net, fishermen for catching their fish in and embroiderers to use as a base fabric for decorative darning and needle-weaving. Netting was also used in the late nineteenth century to make purses, boxes and other small accessories.

Materials required
To make filet net, you will need some basic equipment as follows:
Cotton string, crochet cotton or non-stretch knitting yarn.
A netting needle These hold the string or cotton and vary in width from 12mm (½ in) wide to 18mm (¾ in) wide.
Mesh stick or gauge This determines the size of the mesh. They can be improvised from flat pieces of wood, such as rulers, but ideally, they should be made of perspex and about 15 to 20cm (6 - 8 in) long.
Working base Traditionally, a weighted cushion was used to suspend netting and a substitute can be made from a fabric wrapped brick. Alternatively, use a table clamp, a firmly-fixed hook or a door knob.

Preparation
1 Prepare the working base. Cut a 40cm (16 in) length of cotton yarn and tie a foundation loop to the clamp.
2 Fill the netting needle with cotton yarn leaving a 40cm (16 in) end free for working.
3 Attach the end of the cotton to the foundation loop with a netting knot. (A door knob has been used in Fig 1.)
4 *1st row.* Hold the loop and the gauge between thumb and forefinger and take the cotton yarn round the gauge and the first three fingers, then holding the yarn with the

thumb, take it back behind the fingers and gauge, leaving a loose loop (Fig 1).
5 Take the needle up through the loop held by the fingers, behind the gauge and into the loop. Leave this loop round the 4th finger (Fig 2).
6 Pull the needle through, releasing the loop held by the thumb. Then pull again, releasing the loop round the first three fingers, and finally releasing the loop around the little finger. Pull the thread tight to make a knot (Fig 3).

If a straight row is worked, this method will produce a diamond mesh net. If a square mesh net is required, start with 2 knots on the foundation loop and increase at the end of every row by knotting twice into the last loop.

Continue in this way until there is one more loop than needed for the width of the finished square. Work 1 row without increasing, then decrease 1 loop at the end of every row by working the knot into 2 loops of the previous row, until 2 loops are left on the gauge. To start a new row, turn the netting so that the last loop becomes the first loop of the next row.

Ideas for filet net
Filet net is so secure in construction that it will not fall apart even when cut close to the knots. The ancient Persians used filet to make nets of fine gold thread and then wove them with silken threads. Modern threads are thicker but a gold net could be made, woven with gold ribbons, to make a small bag or pouch. Once you become more practised, you will be able to construct shaped objects, such as hats or perhaps a ball-shaped lamp-shade.

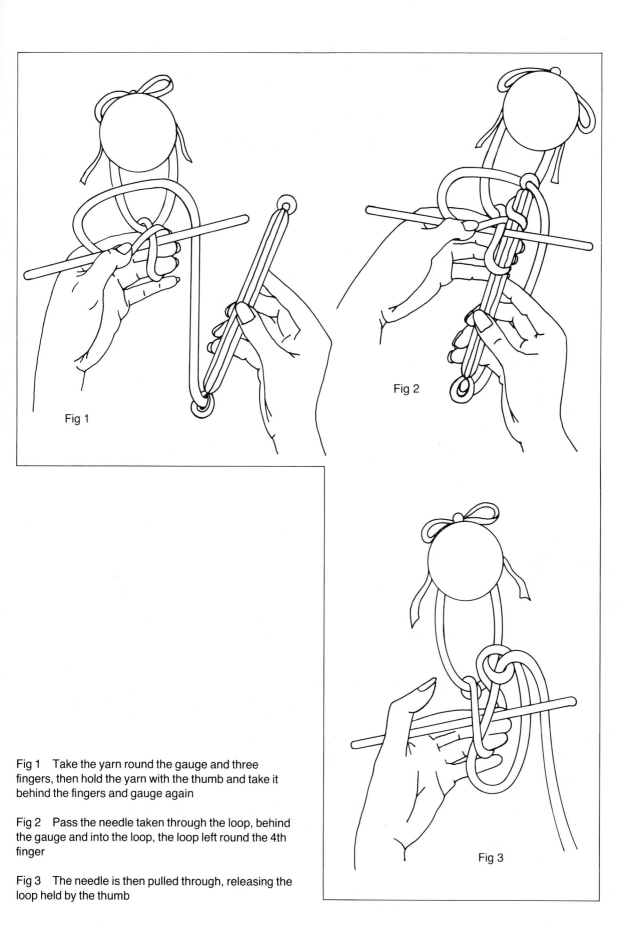

Fig 1   Take the yarn round the gauge and three fingers, then hold the yarn with the thumb and take it behind the fingers and gauge again

Fig 2   Pass the needle taken through the loop, behind the gauge and into the loop, the loop left round the 4th finger

Fig 3   The needle is then pulled through, releasing the loop held by the thumb

Quilted net purse

The soft-looking texture of this purse is deceptive. The woven fabric is, in fact, quite strong and is therefore practical as well as pretty and could be used to make a much larger purse or bag. Tote bags, large, bolster-shaped knitting bags, small make-up or jewellery purses and sewing hold-alls are all possible with this technique. The woven fabric can also be used to make clothing as the quilted finish provides warmth.

Materials required
Squared dressmaker's paper scale 1 sq = 2.5cm (1 in)
23 × 45cm (9 × 18 in) piece of square-mesh net with 3 holes per 1cm (³⁄₈ in)
23 × 45cm (9 × 18 in) piece of 50g (2 oz) polyester wadding
45cm (18 in) piece of 120cm (48 in)-wide lining fabric
3m (3¹⁄₄ yd) of 3mm (¹⁄₈ in)-wide satin ribbon, peach
1 ball of cotton knitting ribbon, pale pink (only half will be used)
1 ball of shiny rayon knitting ribbon, pale pink (only ¹⁄₄ ball will be used)
1 skein stranded embroidery cotton, pink or peach
Pink sewing thread
Small quantity of double knitting yarn, white
2 press fasteners
1 packet bias binding, pale pink (optional)

Preparation
1   Draw the purse pattern from Fig 1 (page 64) onto squared paper, scale 1 sq = 2.5cm (1 in). Trace the patterns onto thin card. Cut out for templates.
2   Use the templates to cut the purse pieces from net, leaving 2cm (³⁄₄ in) extra round each shape. Make sure the straight grain arrow on the pattern aligns with the threads of the net.

Weaving
3   Weave the ribbons and knitting ribbons in a random colour sequence through the pieces of net, in an under 1, over 1 weave. Weave just beyond the area of the template so that the finished pieces of ribbon weaving are larger than the templates.

Quilting the weaving
4   Lay the lining wrong side up on a table. Spread the wadding on top. Arrange the pieces of weaving on the wadding and pin through all thicknesses, round the edges and both vertically and horizontally. Baste through the thicknesses and remove the pins. Work the basting about 4cm (1½ in) apart both vertically and horizontally.
5   Using 2 strands of embroidery thread, quilt through all layers using running stitch. Work short, even stitches and follow the lines of the net. Work 1 row of stitching between every 3 rows of ribbon.

Making the purse
6   Lay the templates on the woven fabric and draw round using a water-proof pen. Stay-stitch just inside the drawn lines using a short stitch. Trim away the excess fabric just outside the stitched line.
7   Bind the top edges of the Gusset and the Purse Front, using bias binding (or cut a 3cm (1½ in)-wide bias strip from fabric).

Right: The quilted net purse and a space-dyed purse. The instructions for making the space-dyed purse are on page 76

8　Pin the Purse Front to one long side of the Gusset from ● to ● (see Fig 1), wrong sides together.

9　Bind, turning 1cm (⅜ in) under at the ends to neaten.

10　Pin the Purse Back to the other long edge of the Gusset, then baste and bind.

11　Thread the knitting wool through 4 75cm (30 in) lengths of the tubular knitting ribbon, 2 matt lengths and 2 shiny lengths. Wrap the ends to neaten them. Work wrapping at 6 - 7cm (2¼ - 2½ in) intervals for decoration.

12　Sew the ends of the stuffed ribbons to the purse corners, two at the front and 2 at the back. Attach press fasteners to the flap.

Tote bag

The pattern Fig 1 can be enlarged for a tote bag. Draw the front piece 38cm (15 in) wide by 45cm (18 in) long. The gusset should be 12cm (4¾ in) wide and 128cm (51 in) long and the back piece 38cm (15 in) wide and 72cm (29 in) long. Make marks 44cm (17½ in) from the bottom edge.

When cutting out the fabric, leave 5cm (2 in) extra round each pattern piece because the fabric will be taken up in quilting. You will need extra ribbons for weaving as follows: allow approximately 2 balls of the shiny rayon knitting ribbon, 6 balls of the cotton knitting ribbon and about 20m (22 yd) of the narrow satin ribbon.

Weave the fabric as for the purse and work the quilting by sewing machine.

Make up the bag as for the purse.

To make the handle stronger, it should be long enough to go round the entire bag, along the gusset. Thread knitting wool through 12 lengths of knitting ribbon. Using a 3-strand plait, plait 6 lengths together. Knot the ends. Starting in the middle of the plait, sew it to the front edge of the bag, along the gusset, along the bottom and up the other side, so that the knot is in the middle of the handle. Work the other 6 lengths in the same way and sew it to the back edge of the gusset to make a doubled handle.

Decorating purses and bags

Although the purse pictured on page 63 is plain in finish, it could be decorated in various ways, depending on the end use (and your taste). The flap could be richly beaded, for instance, or a sequin or beaded ready-

Fig 1　Graph pattern for the quilted net purse, pictured on page 63

Flap　　Back　　Front

Gusset

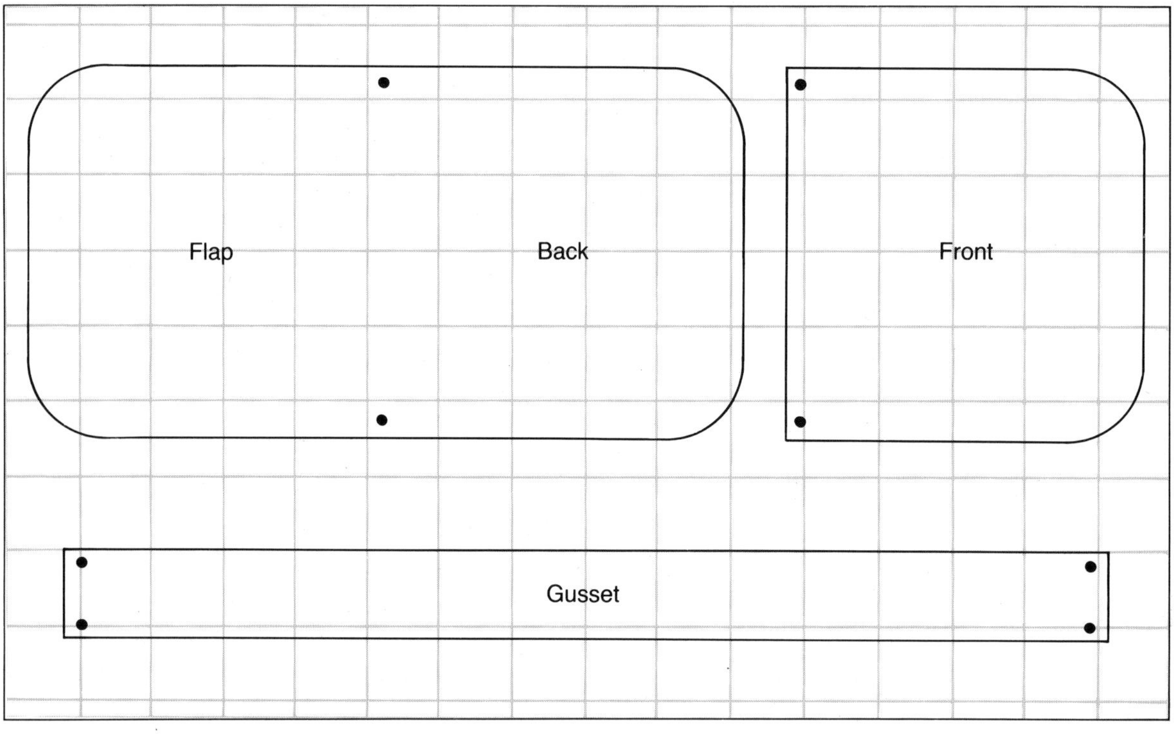

made motif could be sewn to the flap.

The best trimmings for ribbon weaving are, perhaps, made from ribbon and a variety of decorative techniques is possible.

Gathered strips Gather lengths of ribbon by hand or machine, working stitches down the middle of the length or along one edge. Pull up the stitches and sew the gathered lengths along the lines of weaving to cover the bag.

Pleated ribbons You will need a piece of ribbon three times the finished length required. Cut a strip of card 1cm (⅜ in) wide and 10cm (4 in) long. Lay the card 3cm (1½ in) from one ribbon end and fold the ribbon over the card and back again so that the pleat lies on the edge of the card, making a 1cm (⅜ in) pleat. Remove the card and pin the pleat. Lay the card 1cm (⅜ in) away from the fold and make another pleat in the same way. Continue making pleats, which should not overlap each other. Baste the pleats and remove the pins. Sew the pleats to the purse or bag, either in rows down the flap or around the edges, using back stitch.

Folded triangles Cut 15mm (⅝ in)-wide ribbon into 3cm (1½ in) pieces. Fold the top right hand corner to the centre of the bottom edge, then fold down the top left hand corner. Pin to secure. Make a number of folded triangles. Pin to the bag flap in a row, points downwards. Pin a second row overlapping the first row, with the points of the second row lying between the points of the first row. Build up several rows. Cover the edges of the last row with a length of ribbon.

Ribbon net scarf

Ribbon-woven net can also produce light, fragile-looking fabrics suitable for scarves or shawls. The white scarf pictured on page 87 is made of a large-mesh French curtain net (see page 128 for stockists' information). A variety of different ribbons were used for the weaving – satin, taffeta and crepe ribbons and knitting ribbons – together with lengths of knitting cotton.

Materials required
30cm (12 in) of 150cm (60 in)-wide net
An assortment of ribbons, knitting tapes, yarns etc
Long ball-ended bodkin

Preparation
Cut all the ribbons and yarns into 2m (2¼ yd) lengths.

Weaving
Thread each length of ribbon or yarn into the bodkin and weave through the holes of the net, along its length, leaving 25cm (10 in) hanging free at both ends for a fringe. The scarf pictured was worked in an over 2, under 2 weave but this can be varied if you prefer. A pleasing effect might be achieved by 'staggering' rows 2 mesh threads each row and then reversing the pattern to produce a chevron effect. Use the ribbon and yarns in a random sequence.

It is advisable to weave with the net lying flat on a table top and to work only short lengths at a time to avoid puckering the fabric. To vary the texture, some ribbons might be twisted or spaces could be left between the rows of ribbon. Ribbon could also be knotted during weaving.

Finishing the scarf
To finish the weaving, knot 2 or 3 ribbons together at the ends to make a fringe. Slide the knots along a needle so that they lie close to the fabric. Cut ribbon ends off diagonally to minimise ravelling.

Diagonal darning

Diagonal darning is a stitch used in canvas work, and is easily adapted for use with narrow ribbons. It can be worked in one direction or in both directions and can cover the canvas totally or partially.

To work darning, thread the needle with narrow ribbon. Tie a knot in the end. Bring the needle through to the front of the canvas. Weave diagonally across the canvas to near the edge of the area. Take the ribbon under two threads of the canvas vertically or horizontally, bring the needle to the front again, ready to work the second row of darning. Continue working rows in the same way. Take care with the vertical or horizontal stitch at the edges. If this is not worked correctly the second row will be in the wrong place.

Uses for diagonal darning

Diagonal darning with ribbon can be used for bags, purses and belts, book covers and picture frames, and can be set into fabric cushions. In fashion clothes, it can be used to make decorative pockets, yokes and cuffs. In ecclesiastical embroidery, diagonal darning could be worked on burses and for kneelers.

Diagonal darning can be adapted to use on softer nets and meshes, where it takes on a quite different look. Wider ribbons could be used to give a squashed effect, and yarns could be mixed with the ribbons. On a larger scale, the technique can be worked on rug canvas to make cushions and bedside and fireside rugs.

A contrast of scale is often very effective, and diagonal darning can be worked on two or three different sizes of canvas, and combined in one piece such as a cushion. The central square could be worked in the fine canvas, and be inset into the rug canvas which becomes a border. The same ribbons would be used in two or three different widths to emphasise this change of scale. The darning might also be worked in two different directions – one way on the fine canvas, and the opposite on the rug canvas. There could also be a slight colour change as well, so that the border effect is enhanced. Stitching could be worked on the finer canvas, but not on the rug canvas.

Usually, diagonal darning is worked over alternate intersections of canvas and this leaves space for the opposite diagonal to fill in the gaps. However, endless pattern variations are possible by altering the spacing, the colours and whether darning is worked in one or both directions. Here are some patterns to try:

1   One set of diagonals can be worked with a line or darning worked on the straight instead of the second diagonal.

2   Every 3rd or 4th line of darning can be omitted in both directions.

3   Alternate rows, or every 3rd row can be worked in a different colour.

4   Ribbons can be used in one direction and yarns in the opposite direction.

5   An intentional 'mistake' can be made at the edge so that the rows of stitches are no longer parallel to each other, and so a totally different pattern is created.

6   Texture can be used by twisting or looping the ribbons where they lie on top of the canvas.

Metallic threads and ribbons woven through three sizes of silver-sprayed plastic canvas   *Thea de Koch*

Weaving through canvas

Straight weaving through canvas is worked in one direction only, unlike diagonal darning. The canvas should have a large mesh, six to eight holes to 2.5cm (1 in), depending on the size of the article you wish to make, and the width of the ribbons. Very narrow 1.5mm (¹⁄₁₆ in) wide ribbons will lie flat when woven through 4 holes per 1cm (³⁄₈ in) canvas. Obviously, wider ribbons need canvas with a larger mesh.

Ribbons can be woven over and under a single thread of canvas, or under and over two or three, or any combination of these. Hand or machine-stitching can also be combined with weaving and could fill in alternate rows, or whole areas, and provides a contrast of texture.

Basic techniques

Canvas should be mounted in an embroidery frame or tacked to a picture frame to hold it taut while you are weaving, but this is not essential – it can be held in the hand if preferred. If the threads of the canvas appear to show through the weaving, it can be sprayed with car spray paint, or painted with fabric dye. Allow to dry thoroughly before starting to weave.

Use a large bodkin, tapestry needle or a big plastic needle for needle-weaving the ribbons. To start, take the needle through the canvas from the right side about 5cm (2 in) from where you intend to begin stitching. Bring the needle up at the stitching point, leaving a 10cm (4 in) end hanging on the right side. When finishing that length, take the needle through to the wrong side and darn the end under worked stitches. Take the starting end through to the wrong side and darn this in also.

On large items, worked on rug canvas, which has much bigger holes, strips of fabric, or strips cut from dyed nylon tights, could be combined with ribbons and will provide a change of texture.

Canvaswork and weaving cushion

In the partially-worked cushion pictured on page 71, ribbon-weaving through canvas has been combined with satin stitches worked in ribbons of different widths, used for the border. The colour scheme was inspired by a melon flower, and the knitting ribbons have been space-dyed to match the flower's colours. (For space-dyeing, see page 10). Other types of matt and shiny narrow ribbons, tubular and knitting ribbons have been used to complete the scheme, as space-dyed ribbons alone would not have provided sufficient contrast.

Materials required

45cm (18 in) square canvas with 10 holes per 2.5cm (1 in)
4m (4³⁄₈ yd) of 1.5mm (¹⁄₁₆ in) wide ribbon in four colours
3 skeins of knitting ribbon for space-dyeing
3 skeins of tape, (1 shiny, 2 matt)
2 skeins of toning, plain coloured knitting ribbon or tape, 1 matt, 1 shiny
Tapestry needle size 16
Embroidery frame, (or old picture frame) large enough to take the canvas
Feather cushion pad 40cm (16 in) square
Backing fabric

Preparation

1   Mount the canvas on the frame using rust-proof drawing pins. (Alternatively, lace the folded edges of the canvas to the frame,

keeping the straight grain parallel to the frame.)

2 Mark out a 38cm (15 in) square, centred on the canvas, using a permanent colour felt pen in a similar colour to the ribbons. Then mark a 16cm (6½ in) square in the centre of this.

Weaving

3 Threading the ends into a tapestry needle, weave the ribbons and knitting ribbons through the central square in the canvas. Any weaving sequence you like can be used. The sample pictured was worked under 1, over 3, under 1, each row starting 1 hole down. Leave the ribbon ends hanging at the back of the work.

4 When the central square is finished, work bands of satin stitch around the edge until the larger square is filled. Vary the depth of the bands by working over 2, 3, 4, 5 or 6 threads in different rows. Vary the texture and colour of each row also.

Finishing

5 Trim the canvas back to within 12mm (½ in) of the weaving. Cut a piece of backing fabric to the same size. Pin and baste the weaving to the fabric, right sides together. Begin to machine-stitch 5cm (2 in) from a corner, work three sides then 5cm (2 in) of the 4th corner. Snip into the canvas and fabric to ease the corners and turn the cushion cover to the right side. Insert the cushion pad and close the open seam with slip stitches.

Other ideas

The method of weaving described for the cushion cover can be used to make other things where a rigid structure is required – bags, boxes, floor cushions, rugs, lamp bases etc. It is also a different way of covering chair seats and stools, as an alternative to the embroidery on canvas which has been used for centuries. Ribbon weaving will withstand a great deal of wear and can be easily cleaned when required – so your work can look good for a number of years.

When mounting the weaving on stool tops and chair seats, dampen the canvas slightly then pin it over the wooden frame. As the canvas dries it will shrink slightly giving a perfect fit.

Weaving through rug canvas will not only make superb large floor cushions but hard-wearing rugs. Working on this larger scale gives an opportunity for mixing textures and will perhaps encourage you to include some wide strips of fabric and thick, wool yarns in the weaving. Worked as a wall hanging, extra texture such as tassels could be suspended from the weaving.

A smaller scale canvas is used for items such as belts, bags and boxes. For belts, use a double layer of canvas for the weaving and the finished belt will not need lining or stiffening.

There are good commercial paper patterns for making fabric bags which can be adapted for canvas and ribbon weaving. The bags will, of course, require lining. Soft bags could be made from deck chair canvas or mattress ticking and a ribbon woven inset could be introduced.

Even luggage can be worked with ribbon – large saddlebag or satchel shapes in canvas provide opportunities for weaving.

Boxes made of fine-mesh canvas make charming and unusual gifts. Care must be taken to see that corners are square and that lids fit well. Although ribbon weaving can be worked all over the surface, you might also try the effect of a small woven inset in the lid and apply a luxurious fabric, such as velvet or needlecord, to the box sides and base.

Mirror frames are another possible project for ribbon and canvas. After completing the weaving, lace the canvas over thick card and glue a mirror to the woven surface. Back the mirror with a piece of fabric, hemming the edges to the ribbon weaving.

Free-standing ornaments, such as lamp-shade bases and pretty waste baskets can be made by covering an existing base with a piece of woven canvas. Oversew the edges together and cover the top and bottom edges with decorative braid.

Stitching on canvas

There are two ways of stitching on canvas before weaving the ribbons through it. In the first, straight lines are stitched between the canvas threads, and in the second, machine zigzag stitch is worked over the threads.

Straight stitching

Set the sewing machine to normal tension and a stitch length of 2. Using machine-embroidery thread, machine-stitch between 2 threads of the canvas. The foot can be kept on if you wish, but it is easier to see what you are doing if you take the foot off altogether. Work 4 or 5 rows of stitching close together until the space between the threads is filled.

Keep to one bobbin colour when working a strip of stitching otherwise the effect will be lost. Work down alternate lines of the canvas, every third line, or haphazardly, leaving empty spaces to weave the ribbons through afterwards. Colour can be varied by changing the bobbin thread colour for the different strips. Different coloured threads can be worked across the canvas and colour changes can be emphasised by using ribbons in the same colours. Stitching can also be worked on the diagonal.

Zigzag stitching

Zigzag stitching on canvas can be used in two ways. In the first, a single thread of canvas is covered with stitchery and in the second a wider stitch is worked which covers two threads of canvas.

Method 1

Set the sewing machine to a normal tension, a short stitch length and to a width of 2 or 3, depending on how thick the canvas threads are. The stitch must comfortably clear them.

The machine foot can be left on or removed. Machine-stitch along the canvas covering the selected thread with stitching. At the end of the row, turn the canvas and work back along the next thread.

Method 2

Set the sewing machine to the widest zigzag stitch and to normal tension. Position the machine needle in a hole of the canvas and then commence stitching in a straight line, covering two threads of canvas. A single, solid row of stitching can be worked, or 'blobs' of stitching between the horizontal threads of canvas. The stitches should be close enough to cover the canvas, but not so close that they pile up on each other.

Alternative threads

Although fine machine-embroidery threads have been suggested for these techniques others can be tried. A fine wool thread may be able to be passed through the needle and metallic threads look very rich. Matt wool threads might be combined with shiny rayon threads, and the ribbon weaving afterwards worked in matt and shiny ribbons also.

Canvas for ribbon weaving

Canvas should have at least 10 holes per 2.5cm (1 in) otherwise you will not be able to weave the ribbons through it. Rug canvas, with larger holes, can also be used.

There are various plastic canvases available which can be stitched upon, and a millinery canvas called 'Breton net' is pleasant to use as it is rather more delicate. For experimental work, try stitching on stiff nylon grids or metal and wire meshes.

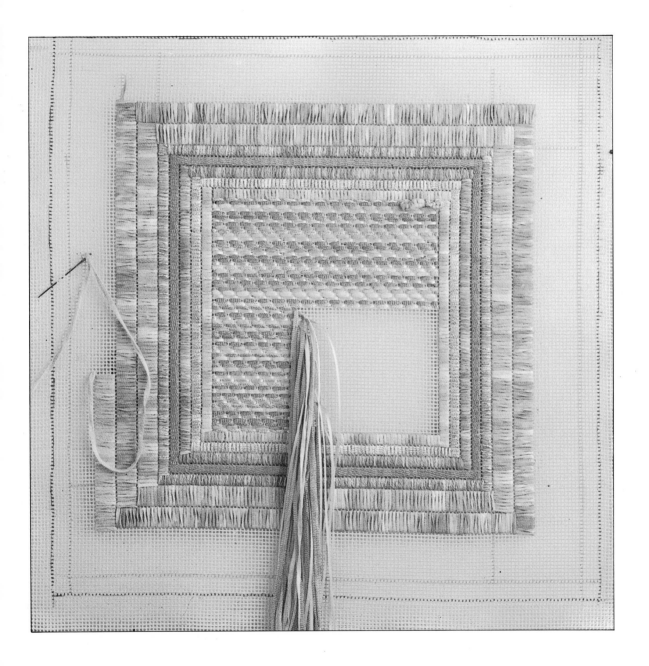

Weaving through canvas with stitchery

This is an extension of the technique of weaving through canvas described on page 68 and the effect is very much richer. Machine-stitching is worked along some rows of canvas before the weaving is worked. Any machine-embroidery thread can be used and four or five rows of stitching can be worked between two vertical threads of canvas. For the saddlebag purse pictured on page 75, copper embroidery thread was used with different coloured threads on the bobbin – gold, black and brown. The bobbin thread was strong enough in colour to alter the colour of the copper on the top. The canvas was sprayed copper with spray paint before being worked to prevent canvas threads showing through.

Copper saddlebag purse

This small bag holds a surprising amount for its size, and can hang from your wrist or shoulder. This is an occasion for using precious, imported ribbons, or antique ribbons which you have been saving for something special.

Materials required

Squared dressmaker's paper, scale 1 sq = 2.5cm (1 in)

40 × 30cm (16 × 12 in) piece of thin card

40 × 30cm (16 × 12 in) piece of canvas, 8 holes per 2.5cm (1 in)

40 × 30cm (16 × 12 in) piece of lining fabric

40 × 30cm (16 × 12 in) piece of light-weight iron-on non-woven interfacing

3.55m (3⅞ yd) of string approximately 3mm (⅛ in) wide

2 reels of variegated metallic machine-embroidery thread

½ ball or 1 skein of knitting ribbon

2m (2¼ yd) of 1.5mm (1/16 in)-wide metallic ribbon

Preparation

1   From the graph pattern Fig 1, draw the pattern pieces onto squared paper (scale 1 sq = 2.5cm (1 in) and then trace the shapes onto thin card. Cut out the patterns for templates and mark in the dots.

2   Hold the templates on the canvas taking note of the direction of the weave and, using a permanent felt pen, draw round the shapes. Cut the shapes from the canvas, leaving a margin of 2.5cm (1 in) all round each piece.

3   Using a long machine stitch, stay-stitch each piece just outside the marked lines to keep them in shape. With the foot on the machine and at normal tension and with a medium stitch length, work over alternate rows of the canvas using the metallic thread. Work 4 or 5 rows of stitching in each row.

Weaving

4   Thread ribbons into a large tapestry needle and weave the ribbons through the unstitched rows of canvas, leaving a short length hanging at each end. The bag pictured is worked with an over 1, under 1, over 1 weave.

5   Work all the bag pieces in the same way.

6   Stay-stitch round each piece again, securing the ribbon ends. Check to see if there has been any distortion by placing the templates on the canvas. If there has, adjust the shape by marking and restitching the edges. Trim to the stitching line.

Lining

Using the templates cut the shapes from the lining fabric and then bond the lining pieces to the worked bag pieces, following the manufacturer's instructions.

Finishing

7 Using the metallic thread in the sewing machine, satin-stitch the top edge of the Bag Front and the edges of the Gusset piece. Satin-stitch round the Front Flap from ● to ● (see Fig 1). Three rows of satin stitch will be required to cover the edge, starting with a medium-width stitch and with subsequent rows a little wider. Trim off any thread wisps after the first row of stitching.

8 Pin the Bag Front piece to the Gusset, wrong sides together, with the straight edges level, placing the pins at right angles to the edges. Baste, then remove the pins and straight-stitch the seam just inside the satin-stitched edge. Work machine satin-stitch along the seam edge as before.

9 Pin and baste the Bag Back piece to the Gusset from ● to ● (see Fig 1), wrong sides together. Stitch and then satin-stitch as before.

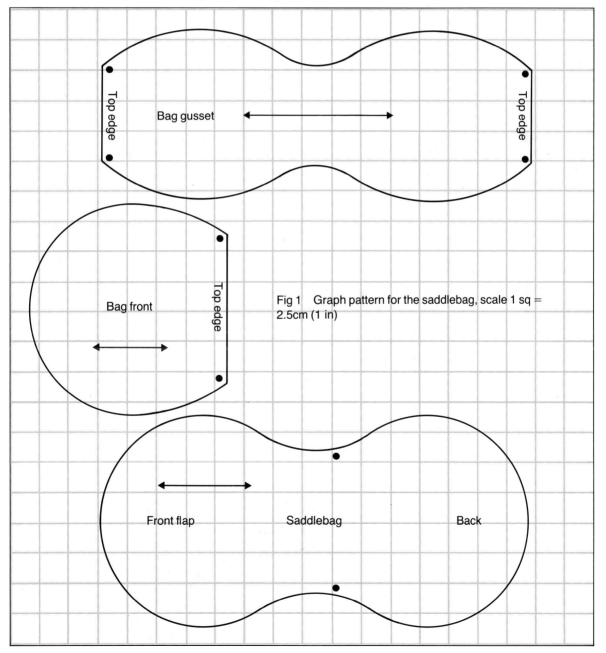

Fig 1   Graph pattern for the saddlebag, scale 1 sq = 2.5cm (1 in)

Handle

10   Place one end of the string under the presser foot of the sewing machine, holding it with the left hand just behind the foot. Lower the machine's foot onto the string. Set the machine to the widest zigzag stitch and work over the string. Three or four rows of stitching will be needed to cover the string.

11   Cut off two 50cm (20 in) lengths of string for the front fastening. Cut the remainder into 2 pieces. Wrap the ends of the short lengths to neaten using metallic embroidery thread. Dip the wrapped ends in PVA glue (it will dry transparent). This will prevent any ravelling.

12   Fold one short piece in half and sew it to the centre of the Front Flap. Fold the second piece and sew it to the centre bottom edge of the bag. Place one end of a long piece on the inside of the front seam at ● and sew firmly in place. Sew the other end to the opposite front seam. Sew the second long piece to the back seam

13   Knot the handles as shown in the picture. Knot the four short ends together to hold the bag shut.

Press fasteners could be an alternative closure or small pieces of touch-and-stick fastening stitched to the canvas.

Variations on the design

In the Saddlebag pictured, the ribbons were woven in an under 1, over 1 weave but the pattern could be varied by weaving under 1, over 2, or 3. Ribbons could be knotted or twisted while being woven. Glass or metallic beads could be sewn on to further decorate the front flap.

Right: Copper saddlebag purse (instructions on page 72). For an alternative colour scheme, use gold thread and spray-paint the canvas gold also

Space-dyed bag

The bag, (pictured on page 63), is made from space-dyed ribbon woven through stitched canvas. Both the ribbon weaving and the stitchery are worked so that the colours shade from pale tones at the top to deeper tones at the bottom edge.

A close-up of the bag's weave can be seen on page 14.

The pattern, Fig 1, could be worked to bigger dimensions to make a shoulder bag and perhaps a wide belt could be made to match.

Materials required

Dimensions: 19.5 × 12.5cm (7⅝ × 5 in), excluding fringe

22 × 44cm (8½ × 17½ in) piece of canvas with 4 – 5 holes to 1cm (⅜ in)

25 × 35cm (10 × 14 in) piece of cotton fabric for lining

Bonding interlining

2 balls of white cotton tubular knitting ribbon

2m (2¼ yd) of white chunky knitting wool

Machine-embroidery threads in the following colours: pale pink, pale yellow, pale green, lilac, mid-blue, soft red, rust, and golden yellow

Red, blue and yellow cold water dyes

Preparation

1   Wind the knitting ribbon into a skein and space-dye it following the technique described on page 10. Dye the lining fabric also. In the bag pictured on page 63, small areas of ribbon and fabric were left undyed to leave white patches.

2   Draw the pattern from Fig 1, following the measurements and trace the shape onto cardboard to make a template.

3   Lay the template on the canvas, the broken line on the pattern Fig 1 aligned to the canvas thread, and mark round the shape with a waterproof pen. Draw 2 shapes, spaced apart.

Stitching

4   Without cutting out the shapes, stitch the canvas, Set the sewing machine to a width 3 zigzag stitch, and to a very short stitch length. Work satin stitch over the threads of the canvas, starting at the top left hand corner. (The stitching lines are stitched to the straight grain of the canvas but lie diagonally across the bag.) Start with a pale colour and work each row as far as the broken line shown on the pattern Fig 1. Use a different colour thread for each row. When the stitching has been worked in one direction, start again at the top right hand corner, again using the paler threads, and then progressing to the darker tones. Work both drawn shapes for the back and front of the bag (both sides should match in colours).

5   Cut out the front and bag pieces just outside the drawn outline.

Weaving

6   Weave lengths of the dyed knitting ribbon through the canvas threads in an under 1, over 1 weave, leaving 1cm (⅜ in) hanging free at the top and 12cm (4¾ in) at the bottom.

The paler areas of the ribbons should be arranged to be at the top of the bag and the darker tones at the bottom.

7   Use the card template to cut out 2 pieces of lining fabric. Bond the lining to the back of the woven canvas pieces.

8   Lay both bag pieces together, wrong sides facing and pin the sides and bottom edges.

9 Thread a length of knitting ribbon into a large-eyed, sharp needle and oversew round the sides and bottom edges, taking care not to catch in the fringe. The stitches should be close together so that the canvas edges are covered.

10 Oversew the top edges of the bag turning the ribbon ends to the inside and catching them in the stitches.

Leave a small loop in the threads at the corners for the handles (see page 63).

11 Thread the chunky wool through 2m (2¼ yd) of tubular ribbon. Cut in 2 pieces. Pass the end of one piece through a handle loop, fold the end back 1cm (⅜ in) and bind with thread to secure. Pass the other end through the opposite handle loop and finish in the same way. Work 2 handles.

12 Cut 4 lengths of ribbon 1m (1⅛ yd) long and push through the loop on one side of the bag and pull through until the ends are even then bind close to the handle. Do the same on the other side of the bag.

Fig 1 Draw the pattern from the measurements given, then cut a cardboard template

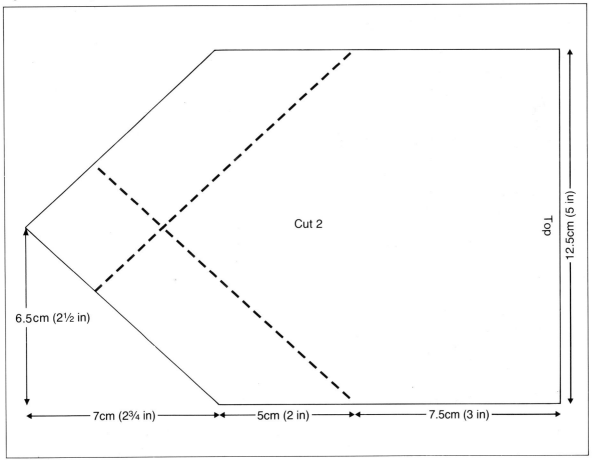

6.5cm (2½ in)

7cm (2¾ in) 5cm (2 in) 7.5cm (3 in)

12.5cm (5 in)

Top

Cut 2

Hot water bottle cover

Many people still prefer the old-fashioned comfort of a hot water bottle to an electric blanket and a cover for the bottle is needed to protect the skin from excessive heat and which is soft and comforting to the touch.

The bottle cover pictured on page 35 is made from fabric through which ribbons have been woven. The fabric was chosen because it had spaced bands of holes but if a similar fabric is not easily obtainable a fabric with an open mesh could be used instead. In this case, you may need more ribbon than is recommended here. To calculate quantities, count how many extra lines of weaving there will be and from this you will be able to estimate the extra length of ribbon required.

Materials required

Thin card
35 × 48cm (14 × 19 in) piece of openweave
  fabric
35 × 48cm (14 × 19 in) piece of 50g (2 oz)
  polyester wadding
35 × 48cm (14 × 19 in) piece of soft cotton
  fabric for backing
Ribbons 3mm (1/8 in)-wide as follows: 1.10m
  (1 1/4 yd) of pale pink; 1.10m (1 1/4 yd) of
  lilac; 1.50m (1 5/8 yd) of peach; 1.50m
  (1 5/8 yd) of pale yellow
2m (2 1/4 yd) of 3mm (1/8 in)-wide ribbon for
  ties
Matching sewing threads
1.40m (1 1/2 yd) of cotton bias binding

Preparation

1   Draw a pattern from Fig 1 (scale 1 sq = 5cm (2 in) and trace onto card to make a template. (Alternatively, place a hot water bottle on the card and draw round the shape. Measure 3cm (1 1/4 in) from the line and draw another line all round, except along the mouth edge of the bottle. Cut out the shape for a template.)

2   Mark equidistant points on both 'shoulders' for the tie positions.

3   Place the template on the openweave fabric and mark round it with chalk. Move the template and mark another shape.

4   Cut 8 pieces of ribbon 25cm (10 in) long for ties and put them on one side.

Weaving

5   Cut the remaining ribbons into 37cm (14 1/2 in) lengths and, threading them into a blunt-tipped tapestry needle, weave them through the fabric (see picture on page 35 for the colour scheme). Weave both sides of the bottle cover to match.

6   Trim the ribbon ends just outside the outline.

7   Lay the backing fabric flat on a table, right side down. Lay the wadding on top. Spread the woven fabric on top, right side up. Pin through all layers on the edges then through the middle vertically and horizontally.

8   Set the sewing machine for straight stitching at normal tension and with a medium-length stitch. Quilt through all the layers working straight lines from top to bottom and always stitching in the same direction. In the cover pictured on page 35, the stitches are worked either side of the interwoven ribbons. Remove the pins as you work.

9   Cut out the two quilted shapes 6mm (1/4 in) from the marked outline. Bind the top edge of both pieces from shoulder to shoulder.

10   Place both quilted pieces together,

wrong sides facing, and pin together through all layers.

11 Take the reserved ribbon lengths and pin 2 ribbons to each shoulder, 2 on the front and 2 on the back, at the points marked on the template.

12 Bind all round the cover catching in the ribbon ties.

Other ideas
The pattern, Fig 1, can also be used to make a hot water bottle cover of quilted ribbon weaving, or ribbon-woven soft net might be used, interlining the cover with a soft wool fabric for cosiness.

The technique used here, where ribbons have been woven through an openweave fabric, can be used to make similar articles where softness and heat retention are required, such as tea and coffee pot cosies. The graph pattern for the egg cosy on page 49 could be adapted by increasing the scale.

Fig 1   Graph pattern for the hot water bottle cover scale 1 sq = 5cm (2 in)

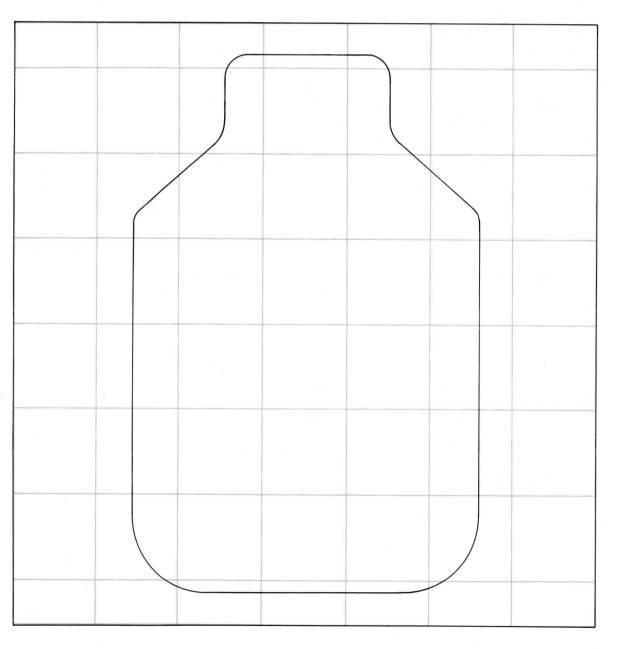

Making cords and tassels

All kinds of articles need cords to finish them off. Bags have handles, of course, but cushions can have loops of cords at the corners as a decorative finish and, for both purses and garments, cords can be threaded through buttonhole loops as a form of closure. There are many methods of making cords with threads, but those described here are particularly applicable to ribbons.

The cord method you use depends on what looks best with the article and whether the cord is to be decorative or is intended to be load-carrying as for a bag. The same type of ribbon should be used for the cord as for the weaving and the same type of embroidery thread as that used for the stitching. If the weaving is very simple a spiral cord could be used as a contrast. If the weaving is complex, then a plainer cord would look better.

Stitched piping cord
Machine-stitching over piping cord is easy to do, and the result makes an extremely strong cord. Thread the bobbin and the needle with the same colour thread and set the sewing machine to the widest zigzag stitch. The stitch length should be about 1 (rather short). Place a length of piping cord under the presser foot and zigzag stitch over it. At the end turn the work while it is still on the machine, and work back again. Four or five workings will be needed to cover the cord. If a pattern begins appearing in the stitching, alter the stitch length slightly. Wrap the cord ends to neaten them. If the cord is being used as a handle, simply tuck the ends into the seams. This cord combines well with machine-stitched ribbons. The same technique can be worked with string instead of piping cord.

Crocheted cords
Crochet a simple chain using narrow ribbon keeping the loops fairly loose. A crocheted chain cord can also be made using two or three 1.5mm (1/16 in)-wide ribbons together. Thread the ribbon end through the loop and pull tight to secure the knot.

Knitted cords
Using 1.5mm (1/16 in)-wide ribbon and double-ended needles, cast on 2 stitches. Knit on these two stitches in plain stitch but do not turn the work. Push the two stitches up to the working end of the needle and knit the two stitches again pulling the working ribbon firmly to the first stitch. Proceed, without turning the work until the cord is of the required length. To finish, knit the two stitches together and pull the end of the ribbon through the loop tightly.

Stuffed ribbons
Thread a tubular knitting ribbon with a chunky knitting wool to make a rouleau. Wrap the stuffed ribbon at intervals with a coloured or metallic thread to add interest (Fig 1). Two or three ribbons can be wrapped together to make a strong handle for a bag. Wrap ends to make tassels.

Wrapped cords
Ribbon can be wrapped round string or piping cord in a spiral, each round slightly overlapping the preceding ribbon. Keep the ribbon in place by wrapping at intervals with embroidery thread. Ribbons 6mm (1/4 in) and 9mm (3/8 in) wide are suitable.

For a variation on the method, dye or paint the piping cord first, then wrap a very narrow ribbon round it leaving spaces between to

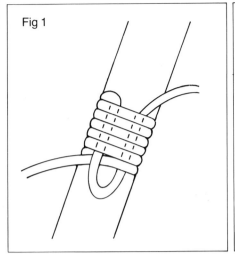

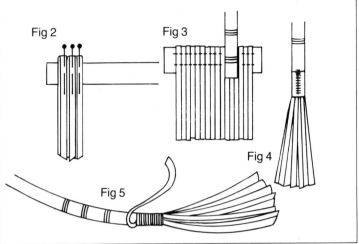

show the cord. Another ribbon could be wrapped from the other end. Finish off cords wrapping firmly for about 1cm (⅜ in), using a matching or contrasting embroidery thread.

Ribbon tassels

Cut narrow ribbons into 15 – 20cm (6 – 8 in) lengths. Fold in half. Pin the folded ribbons to another, wider length of ribbon edge to edge. Machine-stitch the ribbons to the ribbon strip. Wrap the strip of ribbons around a cord end and sew to secure. Wrap with either ribbon or thread (Fig 2–Fig 5).

Knotted cords

Knot three or four lengths of 1.5mm (¹⁄₁₆ in)-wide ribbon together at intervals to make a cord. This looks particularly well with weaving where ribbons are knotted while being woven. The cord is quick to make, and can be either quite thin, using only three ribbons, or thicker using 6, 8 or 10 ribbons.

Spiral cords

Thread a long length of 1.5mm (¹⁄₁₆ in)-wide ribbon into a blunt-tipped needle and work blanket stitch over a length of piping cord. As you work, the stitches will automatically spiral round the piping cord, which gives a very decorative effect. Stitches can be

Fig 1   Wrap stuffed knitting tubing with thread or very narrow ribbon
Fig 2   Pin folded ribbons to a wider ribbon Fig 3, machine-stitch the ribbon and sew round a length of stuffed tubing or a piece of cord. (Fig 4). Bind the top of the tassel with thread or narrow ribbon (Fig 5)

adjusted to become looser or tighter, depending on the effect required.

Plaited ribbons

Ribbons can be plaited together to make a 'cord' which can be used for weaving through other ribbons, or applied as a trim. As plaited ribbon is flexible, it can be applied round curved edges. Plaited ribbons also make good belts, hair-bands, neck ties etc, and strong straps for bags and purses. Two kinds of plaits are possible, a flat plait and a folded plait (Fig 6 and Fig 7).

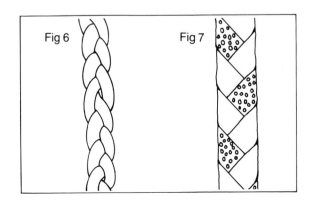

Fig 6   Work the flat plait bringing ribbons forward without folding. For Fig 7, fold the ribbons forward at each stage

Woven spool knitting

Spool knitting is worked on a tool, sometimes called either a 'Knitting Nancy' or a 'French Knitter' and these are available from craft shops and some shops selling knitting wool and accessories.

A small knitting spool can also be made from an empty wooden spool (Fig 1) or from a large cork with a circular hole cut through. A larger spool could be carved from a piece of wood.

Spool knitting is a simple form of frame knitting and is worked as follows:

1   Knot the yarn to a nail (or to the hook) at the top of the spool (Fig 1). Loop the yarn end round the nails (or hooks).
2   After the second winding, lift the lower loops over the nails or hooks, towards the hole, using a blunt-tipped needle (Fig 2).
3   Continue like this looping yarn round the nails or hooks on each round, with the cord disappearing down the central hole, until the cord is the length required. To finish, lift the loops off the nails or hooks and thread the yarn end through them. Pull the thread

tightly and knot. Usually purchased spools have only four knitting hooks but if you are making your own spool, you can have more nails and knit thicker cord.

Spool-woven cord
The hair decoration pictured is worked over piping cord. The spiral pattern comes automatically as you work, and is then emphasized with ribbons and gold threads.

Materials required
Approximately 1m (1⅛ yd) long (not including tassel)
3 reels of gold or coloured machine-embroidery threads
A spool knitter
1.20m (1⅜ yd) of thick piping cord
8m (8¾ yd) of 1.5mm (1/16 in)-wide ribbons
8m (8¾ yd) of gold or coloured embroidery ▶

Fig 1   A knitting Nancy can be made from a wooden cotton reel and four small tacks or nails.
Fig 2   The knitting Nancy: lift the lower loops over the hooks towards the hole, using a blunt-tipped needle

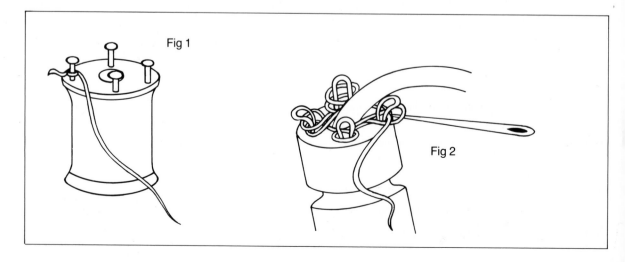

Fig 1

Fig 2

thread, (about the thickness of 3 or 4 ply knitting wool)
A large blunt-tipped needle
Extra 1.5mm ($^{1}/_{16}$ in)-wide ribbon for a tassel

Preparation

1 Take the ends of all three machine-embroidery threads and pull them through the hole in the centre of the spool knitter (a crochet hook might help).

2 Insert the piping cord down through the hole.

3 Cut the thicker embroidery thread into 4 equal lengths. Hold together and, using them as one thread, cast on according to the instructions given.

Knitting

4 Work knitting so that it forms round the piping cord, with the hanging threads equidistantly positioned.

5 Continue knitting until the end of the cord is reached. Cast off.

6 Tie the ends of the threads at both ends of the cord so that it is covered. Trim the cord if necessary.

Weaving

7 Cut the ribbons into 4 equal lengths. Using a blunt-tipped needle, weave the ribbons through the cord, following one stitch line at a time, so that the ribbon spirals, leaving 20cm (8 in) of ribbon hanging free at both ends. As you weave, leave spaces between the ribbons, and then weave the thicker embroidery threads through them.

8 To make the tassel, thread 2 extra lengths of ribbon through the ends of the cord, and wrap the top of each tassel just under the end of the cord. Trim the tassel ends.

9 Wrap the cord at intervals to add areas of colour if desired. (Instructions for wrapping are on page 81).

More ideas

The method of weaving ribbons through spool knitting can be used for items other than belts and jewellery. A single cord will make a handle for a bag or could edge a cushion. Two, three, or even six cords can be twisted together to make a tie-back for a curtain. A single cord, looped on itself and wrapped to hold it in shape could make a blind pull. Two or three cords laid flat and another ribbon woven backwards and forwards through them makes a flat braid which could make a strong camera strap or a belt. The ends would need to be stitched to secure them.

Two or three cords make versatile jewellery, worn as a long necklace tied at the front, or as a choker, bracelets or armbands. They can also be worn as a belt, perhaps knotted together at intervals along the length. Make belts about 2m (2¼ yd) long.

A single cord can be woven through a wide meshed net as a contrast to a flat ribbon, and the item finished off with the same cord. In fashion knitting, cords can be woven through eyelet holes, the ends knotted and with fringe ends hanging.

If the spool-made cord is made with a fine thread or yarn, the loops of knitting will take woven ribbons easily. Do not use too thick a yarn, because the stitches will close up, leaving insufficient space for the ribbon.

Weaving through knitting

Knitting, whether done by hand or machine, makes a soft pliable fabric to weave ribbons through. Knit-weaving, worked on a knitting machine, is a stitch which automatically weaves yarns or ribbons through the surface of the knitting. This can also be done by hand using two needles. Special needles are available which makes the whole hand process easier and instructions for this method are given.

Both hand and machine knit-weaving can be threaded through with ribbons after the knitting is finished through holes, ribs or cables. This is effective for fashion clothes, sweaters, waistcoats and jackets, shawls etc, and for items such as cushions and baby bed covers. Work small samples first to find the correct tension for the fabric before starting a larger piece, as knit-weaving tends to tighten the fabric a little.

Machine knitting

Apart from knit-weaving, ribbon can be woven through many of the basic lace and tuck stitch patterns that punch card knitting machines do automatically. The following pattern requires no attachments and can be worked on any knitting machine.

Cast on using alternate needles. Knit stocking stitch at a very loose tension. Cast off. Pin the knitting out on a board, spray it with water and leave to dry. Weave the ribbons through while the knitting is still pinned to the board. The weaving holds the knitting in shape but it is still inclined to curl at the edges, as does all stocking stitch.

Christmas tree ornaments

Pretty baubles can be made with the knitted fabric. Do not pin it out after removing it from the machine. Sew the knitting round a polystyrene ball so that it is held tautly. Weave narrow Lurex ribbons through the knitting from the top end of the ball leaving the ribbon ends hanging at the bottom to make a tassel. Sew a loop of thread to the top to hang the ball.

Hand knitting

There are many openwork and lacy stitches that can be woven with ribbons. Lace faggot stitch is only one of them.

Lace faggot stitch

Cast on an even number of stitches. P1 * yarn over needle, p2 tog. * Continue from * to * until the end of the row. Repeat for every row. Cast off.

Pin the knitting out on a board, spray it with water and leave to dry. Weave the ribbons through while the knitting is still pinned out.

Garter stitch

Use one size 10 needle and one size 0 needle. Cast on any number of stitches and work garter stitch using the needles alternately for each row. Pin the knitting out on a board, spray with water and leave to dry. Weave the ribbons through while the knitting is still pinned out.

Stocking stitch

Work stocking stitch on very large needles, and weave ribbon through the spaces.

Hand knit-weaving

Knit-weaving by hand gives a very soft fabric which is firmer than ordinary knitting, and does not roll at the edges. The basic structure is usually made with a fine or medium-weight yarn, and narrow satin or taffeta ribbons, or knitting ribbons, flat or tubular, can be used for the weaving. The fabric makes up well into jackets, skirts, baby bed covers, blankets and ponchos and ruanas.

Knit-weave needles

These are hollow needles designed to hold the ribbon which is woven through the knitting. To use them, insert the threader provided into the hole at the point of the needle and push it through to the end of the needle. Thread narrow ribbon through the loop and pull the threader back. Once threaded, pull the yarn out of the loop. Thread the second needle in the same way.

When threaded, the ends of the ribbons should hang out of the holes at the front of the needles. The length should be the same as your chosen width of knit-weaving.

Using double knitting wool, cast on stitches as usual. Ribbon 1 now lies singly in the cast-on row. Push the stitches back a little so that the needle hole is visible. Work the 1st row, knitting the first stitch of the row together with the ribbon protruding from the hole on the left hand needle. This must be done at the beginning of each row.

Ribbon 1 now automatically feeds itself doubled into the cast-on row and ribbon 2 lies singly in the first row.

To begin the 2nd row, pull out ribbon number 1 until it equals the width of knitting. Continue as for row 1.

Although these instructions are for garter stitch, stocking stitch and rib, moss or cable patterns can be worked equally well.

When starting each row, pull the knitting out to the correct width, making sure that the woven ribbon lies evenly along the row. Adjust if necessary. Use any normal knitting pattern, but work a sample first as the weaving is likely to alter the tension.

Kombi needles

These needles are smaller and have an eyelet hole half way along the length.

Using any yarn up to double knitting, cast on. Double the ribbon about 50cm (20 in) from the end and thread through the eyelet. Push the stitches back over the eyelet until the ribbon is visible at the beginning of the row. Remove the ribbon from the eyelet and push the stitches, together with the ribbon, back to the front of the needle again. Fasten off the ribbon by knitting the first stitch and the ribbon together.

Work 2 rows. Repeat as row 1.

As both needles have eyelets, weave the ribbons into every row.

Knit-woven jackets

Because knit-weaving is firmer than standard knitting, it is ideal for making jackets. As the edges do not roll extra layers and pieces can be applied to the basic fabric to add surface interest or warmth. Choose a simple commercial paper pattern such as a design with an easy bat-wing sleeve. The back and fronts could be made in knit-weaving, then strips and squares in different colours or texture added for pockets or shoulder pieces. Contrasting strips could be applied down the front and centre back, or across the yoke.

The main jacket could also be worked in basic colours and then extra pieces worked in different colours for a quick change of look. Pieces can be attached with cords and loops, or with small pieces of touch and stick fastener. The basic fabric could also be hand-woven using stuffed ribbons of a stronger, contrasting colour. The ends of these can be worked into the back of the work, or could hang down the garment for decoration.

Right: Three crocheted bags worked in stuffed knitting ribbons (instructions page 90). The scarf, left, is made by weaving ribbons through net (page 65) while the coverlet (right) is worked with variegated wool and white ribbon on a knitting machine (page 88)

Two projects in knit-weaving

Knit-weaving can be worked by hand using special needles or on a knitting machine. The ruana (a kind of stole), illustrated in Fig 1, is made in one piece but it could also be made in two strips sewn or crocheted together along part of the length. An assortment of different yarn types can be used. Remember that the ends must be darned in at the sides when knit-weaving is completed.

It is difficult to assess the quantity of yarns required as different fibres and qualities make up in different ways. As a rough guide, you will probably find that you need about 600g (24 oz) of yarn and 6 spools of knitting ribbon.

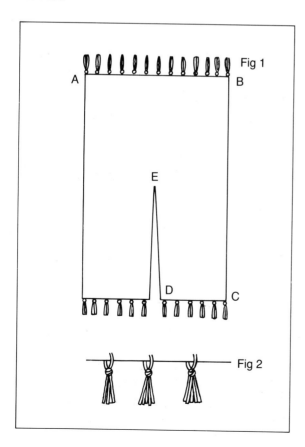

Working by hand

The Addi knitweave needles are recommended for the project (refer to stockists on page 128).

Work the back as one piece up to half way. Then divide the stitches equally and work the front sections separately.

Crochet an edging from the inner lower front corner to the back of the neck and down to the other front cover. Work a knotted fringe along the straight edges using yarns and ribbons (Fig 2).

Working on a knitting machine

On either a standard or chunky knitting machine, set the controls for knit-weave and insert a 2 × 2 punch card. Using yarn and ribbon, work samples on 2 or 3 different tensions with the ribbons going backwards and forwards along the rows. Choose the tension which seems most suitable and calculate the number of stitches required and the number of rows to be worked. Make 2 lengths of knit-weaving to the same measurement. Seam half-way and finish with a hand-worked crochet edging.

Baby coverlet

The baby coverlet is pictured on page 87 and is worked with variegated wool under white ribbon.

Materials required

Dimensions: 50 × 65cm (20 × 25 in)
100g (4 oz) variegated 4-ply knitting yarn on a cone

Fig 1   Make the ruana as shown, A – B measures 120cm (48 in), B – C measures 180cm (71 in) and D – E measures 90cm (36 in). Knot a fringe as shown in Fig 2 using narrow ribbons or knitting yarn

1 reel of 1.5mm ($^1/_{16}$)-wide white ribbon
An assortment of shiny and matt knitting ribbons and textured yarns, all white

Tension
26 sts = 10cm (4 in) at machine tension 6: 44 rows = 10cm (4 in) on a standard knitting machine

Making the coverlet
Cast on 140 sts.
Knit 10 rows in stocking stitch at tension 4.
Set the machine for knit-weaving using a 2 × 2 punch card.
Change to tension 6.
Work 275 rows, weaving a different length of ribbon or yarn in every row. Thread it through by hand leaving 25cm (10 in) hanging free at both ends of every row.
Change to tension 4 and knit 10 rows in stocking stitch. Cast off.

Finishing
Using 4-ply yarn, turn the hems to the wrong side and neaten with herringbone stitch. Knot the side fringes in groups of 5 or 6 strands. Trim neatly.

Thread single lengths of ribbons and yarns into the hems at the top and bottom of the coverlet and knot as before. Trim. (The top edge can be left without a fringe.

Pin out the coverlet to the correct measurements, spray lightly with cool water and leave to dry naturally.

Ribbon weaving through crochet

Like knitting, crochet can produce a fabric ideally suited for weaving with ribbon, and, as crochet does not crease it is a good choice for home furnishing items such as cushions, and for garments. Woven with ribbons, crochet takes on a new dimension in texture and colour. Simple openwork patterns and lacy patterns such as filet can be needlewoven with ribbons, the ribbons looped, knotted or tied in bows.

Crocheted lace edgings and borders are not difficult to work and, when threaded with ribbons, make a pretty finish for children's clothes, baby gowns, lingerie etc as well as for bed linens, towels and cushions.

For a different texture in crochet, stuff tubular knitting ribbon with chunky knitting wool and use the ribbon to crochet heavy duty items such as bags, mats and baskets, perhaps even large cushions. The fabric can be threaded with flat ribbons, leather thongs, raffia or more stuffed ribbons.

To estimate the quantity of ribbon required for weaving, count the number of crocheted rows which will be woven with ribbon and then multiply the length of the row by the number of rows. It is advisable to add approximately 5% to the final total as ribbons tends to be 'taken up' as it passes through fabric and you will almost certainly need a little more than estimated.

Crocheted bags
The small bags pictured on page 87 are so quick to make that they can be finished in two or three evenings. The instructions are for stuffed knitting ribbon but if you decide to use a different ribbon, or yarn, choose a crochet hook of a size that produces a closely-textured fabric with your selected material. These bags are particularly effective made of metallic knitting ribbon in two colours, one for the crochet, and one for weaving. The knitting ribbon can be stuffed with yarns of different colours as they show through the tube slightly. ▶

Materials required

Dimensions: 13 × 31cm (5 × 12½ in) approximately

2 × 50gm (2 oz) balls of tubular knitting ribbon

1 ball chunky knitting wool

A blunt-tipped rug needle or bodkin

Crochet hook size 6

To work the crochet

Thread the chunky wool through one ball of knitting ribbon, using the rug needle.

Using the stuffed ribbon, wind the end round a finger twice and then hook the yarn through it. Work 8 double crochet through the ring. Pull the loose end tight to draw the circle together.

1st round Work 2 double crochet in each chain.

2nd round Work 2 double crochet in alternate chains.

3rd round Work a double crochet in every 3rd chain.

4th round Work a double crochet in every 4th chain.

Continue increasing in this manner until the base of the bag is 8cm (3¼ in) in diameter.

Continue working double crochet without increasing until the bag sides are 8 – 9cm (3¼ – 3½ in) deep.

Finish the bag mouth with a round of half trebles to weave the cord through.

Weaving

Thread the second ball of knitting ribbon with wool. Cut off 2m (2¼ yd) for the cord. Weave the remaining knitting ribbon through the fabric of the bag. You can weave round the bag or from top to bottom. Finish the ends by darning them through to the back of the work. Cut the reserved cord ribbon in half and, starting at each side, thread them in opposite directions through the holes round the top of the bag. Wrap the ends to neaten.

Crocheted baskets

Small baskets can also be made with this method. If cotton knitting is used it can be space-dyed first, and then woven with itself or with a plain coloured knitting ribbon.

Materials required

Dimensions: 15cm (6 in) diameter, 7cm (2¾ in) deep

Crochet hook size 6

40m (43¾ yd) of tubular cotton ribbon, threaded with double knitting wool and measured after threading

8m (8¾ yd) of tubular cotton ribbon, threaded with double knitting wool for weaving

To work the crochet

Wrap one end of the knitting ribbon round a finger twice and hook the yarn through it. Work 8 chain into the ring. Pull the loose end tight to draw the circle together.

1st round Work 2 single crochet into each chain.

2nd round Work 2 single crochet into every alternate chain.

3rd round Work 2 single crochet into every 3rd chain.

4th round Work 2 single crochet in each chain.

5th round Work 2 single crochet into every 3rd chain.

Continue the basket sides without increasing, until all the knitting ribbon has been used. To finish, darn the ribbon end in.

Weaving

Using the 8m (8¾ yd) length of stuffed ribbon, weave it in and out of the crochet, working either round the basket or from top to bottom.

Top: Two samples of stitched knitting ribbon woven through knitting. One is black stitched with white, the other white stitched with black

Bottom: Stuffed metallic knitting ribbons woven through loopy crochet stitches

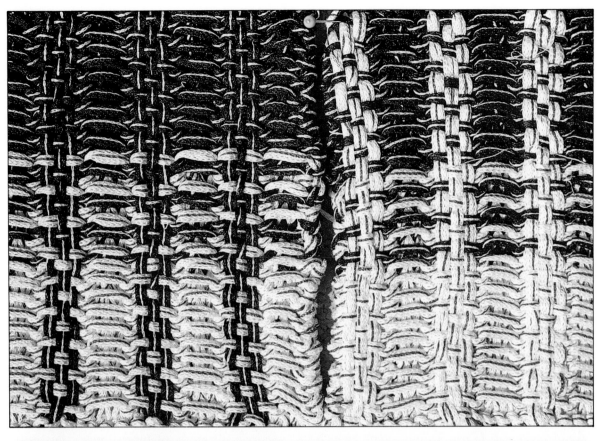

CHAPTER FIVE

Weaving through yarns and stitches

Ribbons can be woven through tautly held yarns or embroidery threads, and this technique has the advantage of leaving most of the ribbons uncovered, so that any pattern or texture can be fully appreciated. To keep the yarns taut enough for weaving through, they can be wrapped around a piece of card (see Bag of Roses, page 106), or wrapped around nails driven into the edge of an old picture frame. Yarns can also be warped onto a bead loom to make long strips of ribbon weaving which can be used to decorate the edges of a jacket or a purse.

Using a table loom, with ribbons woven through chunky or slubbed knitting yarns, a larger piece of fabric would result which could be used for a mat or a bag, or cut into shape for part of a garment. The method chosen for weaving will depend on the kinds of materials used and the size and type of article you wish to make.

Weaving through machine-stitching
If parallel rows of widely-spaced zigzag machine-stitching are worked on fabric, narrow ribbons can be woven through the stitching. A few automatic stitch patterns can also be woven through, but not if the stitches are too close together. Some electronic machines have 'hand-look' stitches which simulate cross stitch, open chain or herringbone stitch, and these are easy to weave through and produce interesting effects.

Weaving through hand embroidery
Ribbons can also be woven through hand stitchery to give a contrast of texture or colour, and to make patterns. The resulting texture can be quite rich and is therefore often better used in small areas such as on bags or cushions, or inset into clothes.

The advantages of modern polyester ribbons – easy care, colourfast, non-shrink and needing no ironing – means that if complementary fabrics and threads are used, the item will launder and dryclean easily and the weaving will not be flattened as it would be if the item were ironed.

Suitable stitches
In canvaswork embroidery, stitches such as cross stitch, Parisian stitch, Gobelin, oblong cross stitch, sheaf stitch and satin stitches can be spaced in working and then ribbon threaded through the stitches. This is a pretty, yet practical, technique and can be used on all kinds of furnishings – cushions, stool tops, chair backs and seats, and on wall panels. The ribbon can be left flat, or looped, twisted or knotted between the stitches to give texture. In freestyle and counted thread embroidery, surface stitches such as blanket stitch, buttonhole stitch, herringbone, wave stitch, chevron and zigzag stitch are just as easy to weave through. The stitches can be worked in free form or massed in bands with the weaving going in straight lines through them. Alternatively, the ribbon can travel up and down between the rows.

If the spaces between the stitches are fairly close together, the embroidery can be used not only for home furnishings but also for fashion accessories and clothes.

Try the effect of buttonhole bars worked fairly close together with ribbons woven in and out of the stitches.

A group of stitches called 'composite stitches', which are worked on bars, can be combined with narrow ribbons to make braids or edgings, or areas of rich texture mixed with plainer areas of stitchery. ▶

Fig 1   Three rows of cross stitch
with ribbons threaded through

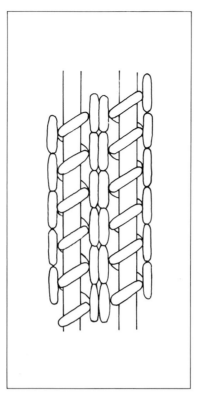

Fig 2   Two rows of chevron stitch
threaded with narrow ribbons

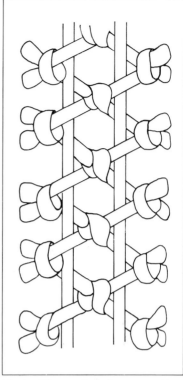

Fig 3   Diamond stitch woven with
narrow ribbons

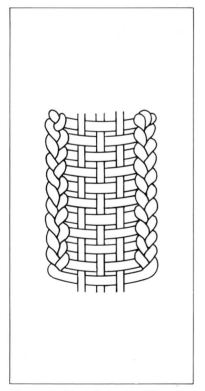

Fig 4   Ladder stitch with ribbons
woven in an under 1, over 1 weave

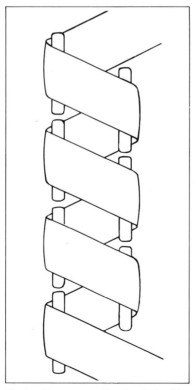

Fig 5   Two rows of back stitch with
ribbon threaded through

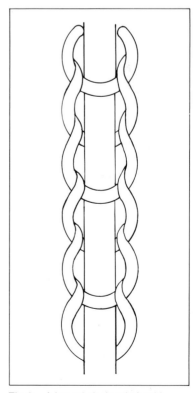

Fig 6   A broad chain stitch with
ribbons threaded through

The choice of thread in this work is important and should contrast with the ribbons. A very shiny rayon thread might look too rich next to a satin ribbon but could be a good choice for a matt knitting ribbon. The gleam of silk could be enhanced by using a taffeta ribbon with it, but be overshadowed by a satin ribbon. The stitch is also important and it is worth working a few samples to find the best combination.

The stitch size must be such that the ribbon is threaded through easily without distortion, so experiment with different sized stitches until you get the effect you want. A very wide ribbon woven through narrow stitches is not necessarily a bad thing however; the ribbon will crush and fold on itself and this is an effect worth trying.

Machine-stitching the ribbon before weaving it through hand embroidery is another alternative and gives not only a firmer 'body' but could also add colour and glitter, if metallic thread is used. If you prefer, work running stitches along the ribbon length. Hand-worked buttonholes, set fairly close together, can also be threaded with ribbon. These could be worked in rows or in a chevron pattern and the resulting fabric might be used for a jacket or for a skirt, or for home furnishing such as cushions.

Insertion stitches

Insertion stitches are used to join two ribbons or the neatened edges of two pieces of fabric decoratively. Stitches include faggoting, buttonhole stitch, herringbone stitch, and ladder hemstitch. The openwork stitches can be woven through with narrow ribbons, and the effect is pretty and delicate on fabrics made of fine fabrics. The technique can also be used on tougher fabrics as a decoration for furnishings, such as cushions.

On fashion accessories, use ribbon-woven insertion stitches to join pieces, such as the front and back of a bag. On table linens, try the effect of a different coloured border, applied with insertion stitches and inter-woven with ribbon.

Pulled, or drawn thread embroidery

Pulled work, sometimes called drawn fabric embroidery, in which the threads of the fabric are drawn together to make holes, can have ribbons woven through the holes in an ordered or random manner. Traditionally, threads match the fabric colour but there is no reason why contrasting threads, and ribbons, should not be used.

A similar technique can also be worked on a machine using a loosely-woven fabric and wide ribbons can be woven through afterwards. Set the machine for darning and frame up the fabric in a machine-embroidery ring. Use a normal tension, and the widest zigzag stitch of which the machine is capable.

Move the framed fabric steadily backwards and forwards while stitching. The stitching pulls the threads of the fabric together, leaving spaces each side of the band of stitching.

This type of embroidery can be worked in a regular or irregular pattern, both of which are easy to weave ribbons through.

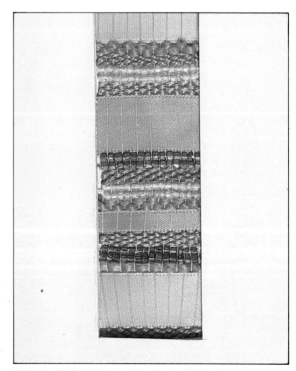

WEAVING ON A BEAD LOOM Satin Ribbons of varying widths, matt and shiny threads, and beads were woven on an embroidery thread warp to make a narrow strip of ribbon weaving. *The author*

GREY AND PINK BAG Different widths of ribbon and tubular knitting ribbon, one piece threaded with chunky knitting wool and thread-wrapped, woven on gold threads over an interfacing. *The author*

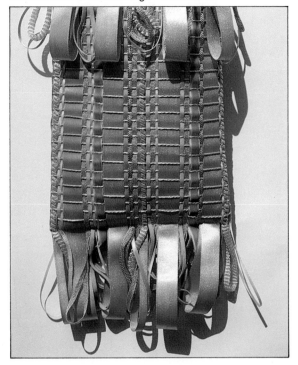

WEAVING OVER VANISHING MUSLIN Narrow ribbons have been woven on a machine-stitched grid worked on vanishing muslin, mounted on sponge-painted fabric. *Betty Marsh*

MACHINE-STITCHING OVER SEQUIN WASTE
Scraps of coloured polythene were glued to paper, then strips of sequin machine-stitched on top. Very narrow ribbons are threaded through. *The author*

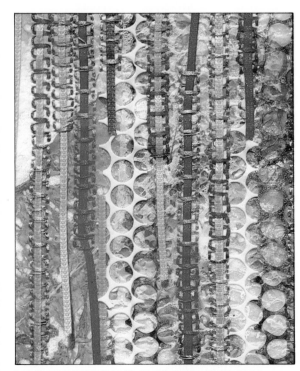

WEAVING THROUGH EMBROIDERY A variegated thread was worked on loose-weave scrim. The frame's movement made the stitch distort the fabric, pulling threads apart for ribbon weaving. *Gail Harker*

Ribbon and drawn thread waistcoat

In drawn-thread work, warp or weft threads are cut and then withdrawn from fabric, and then embroidery is worked on the threads that are left. This technique can be adapted to ribbons, weaving them through the threads instead of embroidering them. Even-weave fabrics with a definite weave, such as linen, coarsely-woven cotton, woven wool fabrics, hessian etc, are used. The technique could be used over a length of fabric which is then made up into a garment. Alternatively, it can be worked as bands and borders on large bags, mats, bedcovers, cushions, and curtains.

Depending on the width of the area of withdrawn threads, any kind of ribbon can be used, to match, or contrast with, the fabric. Textured yarns, stuffed knitting ribbons or metallic yarns can all be used, alone or in combination with plain woven ribbons.

Preparing the fabric

Trim off the fabric selvedges. Decide where the band of withdrawn threads is to be. Mark it lightly with chalk, or with basting threads. Slip the point of a blunt-tipped needle under a single thread of the fabric near to the fabric edge and use the needle to ease up the thread. When the loop can be held in with your fingers, gently pull the thread out of the fabric, easing it as necessary. Continue to withdraw adjacent threads in the same way to the depth of the band.

If only a short band or area in the centre of the fabric is required, withdraw the thread to the edge of the band, then thread the end into a needle weave it back into the fabric. Threads can be drawn in one direction to make bands, or can be drawn both horizontally and vertically.

In the woollen waistcoat pictured narrow ribbons are woven through withdrawn threads in bands, the bands on the front and back lying vertically and on the sides horizontally.

Materials required

For bust sizes 85 – 91cm (34 – 36 in):
Dressmaker's squared pattern paper, scale 1 sq = 2.5cm (1 in)
50cm (20 in) piece of 120cm (48 in)-wide fine tweed fabric
50cm (20 in) piece of 120cm (48 in)-wide lining fabric
8m (8¾ yd) of 3mm (⅛ in)-wide satin ribbon in each of 3 colours, pink, mauve, iris
4 pearl buttons

Preparation

1   From Fig 1, draw the waistcoat pattern pieces up to scale (1 sq = 2.5cm (1 in)) on dressmaker's squared pattern paper. Cut out the pattern pieces and pin to fabric. Mark round each piece with French chalk.
2   Cut out 2 Fronts, 2 Sides and 1 Back (on the fold) leaving an extra 1cm (⅜ in) round each piece for seam allowance. Unpin the paper pattern.
3   Mark the position of the bands on the fabric with basting threads, (The bands are 9mm (⅜ in) wide and are set 4cm (1½ in) apart.
4   Following the technique described on this page, withdraw fabric threads, to the width of the bands (9mm (⅜ in)).
5   Use the pattern pieces to cut out the waistcoat lining pieces.

Weaving

6   Cut the ribbons slightly longer than the

bands. Thread ribbons into a bodkin or tapestry needle and weave them through the fabric. Work an under 6, over 6, under 6, weave in colour 1. Alternate the middle row over 6, under 6, over 6 as shown in the picture, using colour 2. Row 3 is worked as Row 1, using colour 1.

7   Work machine stay-stitching round each piece to secure the ribbon ends. Trim back to the pattern line.

Making the waistcoat

8   Join Fronts to Back at the shoulder seams, right sides facing.

9   Join the Fronts to the Side pieces, right sides facing.

10   Join the Back to the Side pieces, right sides facing. Neaten all seam allowances with zigzag machine-stitching.

11   Make up the lining in the same way.

12   Pin and baste waistcoat and lining together, right sides facing, and machine-stitch all round, leaving an opening at the

Fig 1   Graph pattern for the waistcoat, scale 1 sq = 2.5cm (1 in)

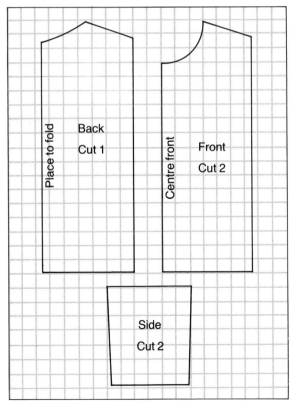

back hem. Turn the garment right side out. Sew up the opening using slip-stitches.

13   Baste round the edges of the garment pulling the stitched seam out with a pin as you go.

14   Top-stitch all round and remove the basting.

15   Fastening tabs: from remaining fabric cut 2 strips 15 × 5cm (6 × 2 in) and 2 pieces of lining to the same size. Stitch the fabric pieces to the lining right sides together on 3 sides, then turn right side out and close the fourth side with oversewing. Press.

16   Make buttonhole loops on one short edge of the tabs. Sew the tabs to the inside front edge of the waistcoat (see picture). Sew on buttons to correspond with loops.

Garments from ribbon weaving

As ribbon weaving is a fabric construction technique, there is no reason – other than cost – why an entire garment should not be made from ribbons. For special, glamorous garments, such as evening jackets and coats, boleros and waistcoats, ribbon weaving would be an adventurous fabric choice. Consider a jacket entirely made of golden yellow ribbons, quilted with gold thread, with a lining in brilliant blue. Or a waistcoat worked in red velvet and red satin ribbons, interlaced with gold ribbons, to be worn with a long velvet skirt or pants. The waistcoat pattern, Fig 1, could be used to make an entire garment from ribbons. Machine embroidery can be worked on the ribbons before or after weaving, and quilting would add warmth, as well as richness, to the finished garment.

Ribbon-woven accessories are often very acceptable to men also; cummerbunds look rich and luxurious and neckties and bowties made from narrow ribbons look extremely smart.

Choosing patterns

When choosing patterns for ribbon-woven garments it is better to select designs with a very simple shape, as few pieces as possible and with the simplest construction details. Darts to not look well in weaving, facings tend to look bulky and button holes are impossible to work neatly. Straight, un-shaped fronts and backs are best, with wide sleeves and T-shaped shoulders.

If there are collar and cuff details, it is better to work these with one layer of ribbon weaving backed with lining than to try and face them with more ribbon weaving.

Hems should be kept as narrow as possible to avoid bulk and it is recommended that all ribbon woven garments be fully lined.

Choosing ribbons

If the garment is to be laundered then the ribbons you use must be washable and colourfast. Choose polyester ribbons which are guaranteed not to shrink, nor colour-run. They will require little or no ironing and this can be an added advantage. Polyester ribbons can also be drycleaned.

Nylon and rayon ribbons are less expensive than polyester but you should test them for colourfastness and washability before applying them to garments. These ribbons usually dryclean, but sometimes steam pressing is used to finish drycleaned garments and ribbons that are not colourfast can spoil a garment completely. Velvet ribbons are available in polyester fibres and these are generally colourfast, but take care with the stronger colours. Gold and silver ribbons, which are a mixture of polyester and Lurex, are usually guaranteed to be washable and dry-cleanable.

When selecting ribbons for weaving a garment trim, choose ribbons in scale to the piece. For small areas such as collars, pocket flaps, pockets and yokes, fairly narrow ribbons – between 6mm and 9mm (¼ in and ⅜ in)-wide will probably produce the best effect.

Larger pieces, such as an inset band on a skirt hem, or a decorative panel set into the back of a jacket, might be worked in ribbon up to 25mm (1 in) wide.

Baby garments are best worked with the narrow ribbons, from 3mm (⅛ in) wide to 9mm (⅜ in) wide.

Choosing the technique

Referring to Chapter Two, you will see that although ribbon weaving over iron-on inter-facing is recommended for most garment trims, the resulting fabric tends to be a little inflexible and this may not be suitable for baby clothes or clothes made of delicate fabrics. Ribbon weaving over a lining fabric produces a softer handle and the technique described on page 24, Fig 3 and 4, is the one you should use for working shaped pieces. The quilting technique described on page 37 could also be used for fashion clothes and accessories and makes a firm yet flexible fabric.

Estimating ribbons for weaving

If you are weaving ribbons through woven fabric or through net or mesh, or other material, it is often possible to measure the piece, row by row, to estimate the total length of ribbon required for the project.

If ribbons are being woven through ribbons to make a large piece of fabric or to the shape of a pattern piece, you will want to be fairly exact in your estimates to avoid wastage.

Estimating for square or rectangular pieces

1 Draw the desired shape to size, including the seam allowance on the matt side of iron-on interfacing.
2 With a soft pencil and ruler, mark the widths of your selected ribbons on the inter-facing, according to the pattern. Mark the ribbons colours and widths A, B, C and so on (Fig 1, page 100).
3 Add the number of A, B and C ribbons, multiplying by the depth of the drawn shape. Fig 1 shows that there are 3 A ribbons, 4 B ribbons and 8 C ribbons. Thus, you would need 3 × 30cm (12 in) for A = 90cm (36 in), 4 × 30cm (12 in) of B = 120cm (48 in) and 8

× 30cm (12 in) of C = 2.40m (2⅝ yd).

The weft is estimated in the same way.

Shaped pieces

To estimate ribbons for a garment, such as a bolero jacket, mark the paper pattern piece with vertical pencil lines to estimate the total length of warp ribbons. Draw lines across the pattern to estimate the total length of weft ribbons. ▶

If you prefer, spread the pattern piece under lightweight iron-on interfacing and trace the pattern piece, then mark in the ribbons (Fig 2, page 100).

Working weaving

Use the pattern pieces as a guide to weaving. If the iron-on interfacing method is being used spread the pattern pieces and lay the interfacing on top. Pin the interfacing to the pattern and then carefully draw over all the pattern lines. Work the ribbon weaving over the interfacing pattern cutting ribbons to fit the shape and thus avoiding wastage (Fig 3, page 101). Complete the weaving as described on page 16. Use the pattern piece to cut the woven fabric. If preferred, the weaving can be stay-stitched on the cutting line before cutting out just outside the cutting line.

Using ribbon weaving

Panels of ribbon weaving worked in brilliant colours and textures can add drama to a garment. They can also add a couture finish, worked in colours matched to the fabric. On delicate garments ribbons add prettiness worked, perhaps, in white, cream or pastel tones.

A baby gown, for instance, in a simple style and fabric, immediately looks expensive and becomes something to be treasured if a yoke of ribbon weaving is added. (Fig 4, page 101). A bridal gown, with an inset waistband of woven pastel-coloured ribbons, finished with streamers to tie at the back, looks original and makes the gown quite unique. This is also an opportunity for co-ordinating bouquet colours to the wedding clothes, and ribbon-woven bible and prayer book covers might also be worked to match (refer to page 48 for the technique).

Study the weaves illustrated on pages 20–21, 22–23 for pattern ideas and choose one suitable for the garment style and for the area of the trim. A simple, plain weave will probably be your choice for an elegant blouse or dress, or for babywear, but one of the other weaves may be more exciting on a high fashionable ensemble. For instance, for shoulder interest on a jacket, consider weaving epaulettes in weaving pattern Fig 7, perhaps knotting the weft ribbons where they cross the warp ribbons.

Linings

Most items require a lining of some sort and these can either be fused to the woven fabric

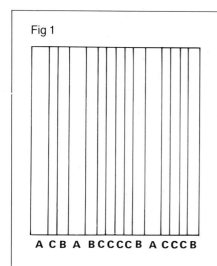

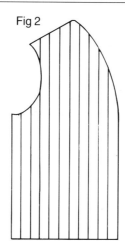

A C B A B C C C C B A C C C B

Fig 1 Estimating ribbon quantities for square or rectangular pieces
Fig 2 Mark the pattern piece with vertical lines to estimate the total length of warp ribbons

or can be made separately and dropped in or attached to the fabric in making up.

If the lining backing method is being used, draw the pattern piece on the wrong side of the lining using dressmaker's carbon paper and a tracing wheel. Pin the fabric to a cork mat and weave over it, following the outline, pinning the ribbons to each other at the edges. When weaving is completed, baste all round on the cutting line, removing the pins. Work a medium-width zigzag stitch just inside the cutting line, then use the paper pattern to cut out.

Fusible web linings
Fusible web is sold with a paper backing.
1   Draw round the pattern piece on the smooth side of the paper, leaving a 3cm (1¼ in) space between each piece.
2   Cut pieces out roughly, leaving extra paper round each piece.
3   Place the pieces with the rough, adhesive side touching the wrong side of the lining fabric. Press firmly with the iron set at 'medium'.
4   Cut out all the shapes on the drawn lines through the paper and fabric together.
5   Peel off the paper. The fabric now has an adhesive surface.
6   Place the adhesive side of the fabric onto the back of the ribbon weaving and press gently until bonded.

Drop-in linings
These are used for items such as bags and purses.
1   Cut a card pattern slightly smaller than the original article.
2   Draw the pattern shape onto the lining fabric, and cut out through two layers of fabric together, leaving a 12mm (½ in) allowance on all edges.
3   Machine-stitch on the drawn line on three sides of the pattern. Trim the corners.
4   Press the seams open but do not turn the article inside out.
5   Fold the seam allowance over the open edge, and pin.
6   Drop the lining into the article, and hem-stitch to the fold on the open edge.

Finishing hems and edges
The group of stitches known as composite stitches which are worked in bars can be combined with ribbon weaving to make braid effects for edgings. The technique can be adapted as a method of securing and finishing folded hems. Fold the hem to the right side of fabric and baste in place. Using a fairly thick yarn matched to the fabric, worked rows of chain stitch through both layers of the fabric, parallel to the edge. Then weave narrow ribbon through the chain stitch loops.

An alternative method is to work the rows of chain stitch first, then a row of blanket stitch over the chain stitches. Weave ribbons through the blanket stitches.

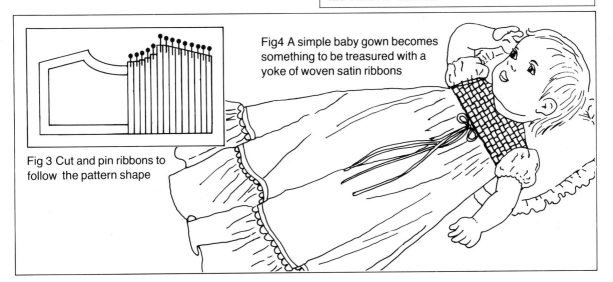

Fig4 A simple baby gown becomes something to be treasured with a yoke of woven satin ribbons

Fig 3 Cut and pin ribbons to follow the pattern shape

Ribbon lampshades

The lampshade pictured is a simple drum-shape with the frame painted white. Ribbons and yarns are wound onto the frame, making a 'warp', and then other ribbons are woven through diagonally. This type of lampshade looks decorative by day and at night, when the lamp is lit, the open weave allows light to show through.

Materials required

Drum-shaped lampshade 18cm (7¼ in) diameter and 17cm (6¾ in) deep
9m (9⅞ yd) of 3mm (⅛ in)-wide ribbon
13m (13⅜ yd) of 6mm (¼ in)-wide ribbon
4.50m (4⅞ yd) of 1.5mm (1/16 in)-wide ribbon
Assortment of silk and cotton embroidery threads and knitting yarns.

Preparation

1   Cut the 3mm (⅛ in) and 6mm (¼ in)-wide ribbons and some of the yarns into 55cm (22 in) lengths. Cut the 1.5mm (1/16 in)-wide ribbon into 72cm (28½ in) lengths.
2   Fold a length of 6mm (¼ in)-wide ribbon over the top of the lampshade frame and tie the ends together at the bottom of the frame in an overhand knot. To keep this knot tight up against the frame, slide a large needle into the loop of the knot before you pull it tight and slide the loop up against the frame. Pull the knot tight with the fingers to keep the ribbon taut.
3   Knot all the lengths of ribbons (except the very narrow) in the same way, spacing them evenly.
4   Fill the spaces between the ribbons with the yarns, knotting them in the same way at the bottom of the frame. (Macrame knots can be varied on some yarns for a change of texture, if preferred.)
5   Leave the ends hanging as a fringe.

Weaving

6   Take a 72cm (28½ in) length of very narrow ribbon over one of the struts intersections at the top of the frame. Take both ends behind the struts to prevent the ribbon from slipping. Weave each end diagonally to the bottom of the frame, towards the next strut along.
7   Knot the ends to secure them.
8   Work all the lengths of very narrow ribbon in the same way.
9   Trim the fringe ends to finish.

For a different treatment, wind the frame of a cone-shaped shade with 2.5cm (1 in)-wide ribbons. Weave a narrow ribbon through, pulling together and knotting 3 or 4 ribbons together. Line the lampshade

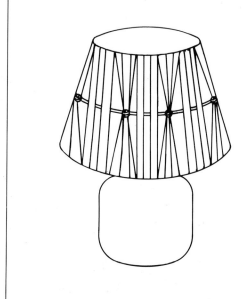

The art of making cushions

Cushions are an ideal way of using special pieces of ribbon weaving, as well as being comfortable furnishings. Well-made cushions should be plump and have clean edges. Here is a method which avoids the 'dog ear' corners which can often spoil the look of a cushion.

When planning the size of the cover, cut the fabric to exactly the size of the cushion pad so that when the seam allowances are taken, the cover is a little smaller than the pad, producing a plump, well-filled look.

Square cushion
1 Draw a pattern for the cushion cover, similar to Fig 1. Round off the corners as shown. Make a card template from the pattern.
2 When the cushion front is completed, place the card template on the wrong side of the fabric and draw round the shape.
3 Pin the cushion back to the front, right sides facing.
4 Starting about 5cm (2 in) from a corner, stitch round the corner, along three sides and then about 5cm (2 in) of the fourth side, stitching on the marked line.
5 Cut out through both thicknesses about 12mm (½ in) from the stitched line. Snip into the seam allowance on the curved corners. Turn to the right side. Push in the cushion pad and close the open seam with slip stitches. Alternatively, a zip fastener or press fasteners can be inserted to close the seam opening. This type of corner looks particularly good with inserted piping.

Flapped opening
Round cushions or those of an irregular shape are more easily finished with a flapped opening, worked on the back of the cushion. This removes the necessity for closing a seam with slip-stitches and is almost as effective as a zip fastener in keeping the cover closed.

1 Cut the completed cushion front to size including seam allowance.
2 Cut the cushion back 10cm (4 in) wider but to the same depth as the front.
3 Cut the cushion back in 2 pieces vertically.
4 Neaten the cut edges of both pieces with a machine-stitched hem.
5 Place one piece over the other, overlapping the hemmed edges so that the cushion back is the same size as the front. Pin front and back together on the edges.
6 Baste, then machine-stitch all round.
7 Turn to the right side and press. The cushion pad is inserted through the flapped opening.
  If preferred, the opening can be finished with ribbon ties or a ribbon loop and button.

Bolster cushion
Bolster-shaped cushions look impressive made from woven ribbons. This is a simple method for making a bolster.

1 Measure the length and circumference of the bolster pad and add 2.5cm (1 in) to both measurements. Weave ribbon to make a piece of fabric to these dimensions.
2 The ends of the bolster can be made from ordinary fabric in a colour chosen to match the ribbons. Cut 2 pieces to the circumference measurement by the diameter of the bolster ends, plus 2.5cm (1 in) on each measurement.
3 Neaten one long edge on each fabric piece by making a machine-stitched casing.

4   Machine-stitch the other long edge to the short edge of the woven ribbon fabric, right sides together (Fig 2).

5   Now join the long edges of the bolster cover, including the fabric ends, in one seam (Fig 2b).

6   Thread ribbon through the casings and draw up to fit the bolster, tying a bow (Fig 3).

Tied bolster

Bolster cushions can also be made with bow-tied ends and if a striped-effect weave is used the finished bolster looks a little like a paper-wrapped candy.

Using a rectangular cushion pad or a small bolster pad. Cut a piece of soft, plain fabric (white looks effective) to the length of the pad plus 20cm (8 in), by the circumference plus 2.5 cm (1 in). Join the two long edges to make a fabric 'tube'. Neaten the tube ends with a narrow doubled machine-stitched hem. Press.

Work a piece of ribbon weaving (using the iron-on interfacing method) to the length of the pad plus 2.5cm (1 in) by the circumference plus 2.5cm (1 in). When weaving and bonding is completed, trim the weaving edges and then turn under a 12mm (½ in) hem all round. Slip the fabric cover on to the pad. Pin the weaving round the bolster overlapping the long edges and pin to the fabric cover all round. Remove the weaving and cover, baste and then machine-stitch the weaving to the cover. Replace the cover on the bolster. Tie ribbons around the bolster ends, gathering up the excess fabric. Tie the ribbon ends in a bow.

If preferred, the ribbon weaving can be worked using the fabric backing method. When completed, join the two long edges right sides facing. Neaten the ends of the resulting 'tube' of weaving with faced hems. Slip the tube of weaving onto the fabric bolster cover. Tie the bolster ends as before.

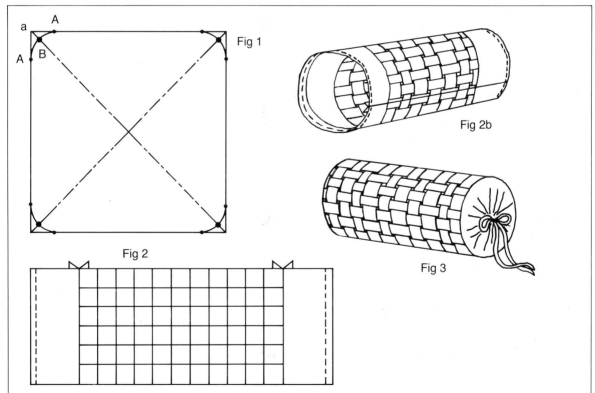

Fig 1   Rounding-off corners: Mark the corners as shown A – A then a – B and round-off A – A

Fig 2   Machine-stitch the pieces of fabric to the ends of the ribbon weaving to make bolster ends. Stitch a casing at the ends

Fig 2b   Machine-stitch the long seam to make a 'tube' for the bolster cover

Fig 3   Thread ribbons through the casings and draw up to fit the bolster cover. Tie the ends in a bow

Bag of roses

To make this bag, the ribbons are woven through an embroidery thread warp so that the rose motifs are not hidden in the finished fabric. Four different rose-patterned ribbons are used for the bag pictured but the pattern can be worked with any short lengths of plain, woven ribbons you may have. Look at the backs of woven ribbons – they can be just as interesting as the front and provide a change of colour.

Materials required
20 × 12.5cm (8 × 5 in) piece of thick card
42 × 27cm (16½ × 10¾ in) piece of pelmet weight interfacing
44 × 28.5 (17½ × 11½ in) piece of lining fabric
1 skein perlé thread no. 3
1 can car spray paint to match ribbons
4 different patterned ribbons as follows:
1.60m (1¾ yd) of (⅛ in)-wide ribbon
1.10m (1¼ yd) of 6mm (¼ in)-wide ribbon
2.60m (2⅞ yd) of 12mm (½ in)-wide ribbon
1.10m (1¼ yd) of 20mm (¾ in)-wide ribbon
10m (11 yd) of 12mm (½ in)-wide ribbon for handle and tassels
1m (1⅛ yd) of thick piping cord

Preparation
Fold the interfacing round the card and pin seams on the two long sides so that the interfacing fits closely. Machine-stitch and then trim the seam allowance. Spray-paint the interfacing on both sides, making sure the edges are covered. Mark dots 6mm (¼ in) apart down both long edges.

Thread the end of the perlé cotton into a needle without cutting it from the skein. Attach the end to the top left edge of the interfacing with a few stitches. Wind the cotton thread around the interfacing on the marked dots and finish with a few stitches at the bottom right corner (see Fig 1, page 29 for technique). Keep the tension even and not too tight.

Weaving
Cut all the ribbons into 51cm (20½ in) lengths. Starting with the narrowest ribbon and using the widths in turn, thread the end into a bodkin.

Beginning at the top edge, weave the ribbon through the cotton threads, over one thread and under the next and so on, working down the bag front, under the bottom edge and up the back of the bag. Leave the ribbon ends loose. Weave all the ribbons in the same way, working a plain weave. Push each ribbon close to that preceding it to cover the interfacing. When the weaving is completed, remove the card lining. To finish the ribbon ends, turn and pin them to the inside, baste and then secure with running stitches worked 12mm (½ in) from the top edge.

Lining
Fold the lining fabric right sides together and stitch the long sides to make a bag. Trim the seam allowances and slip the lining into the bag. Turn in the top edges and slip-stitch.

Handle
Wrap the piping cord with ribbon following the instructions Fig 1, page 81. Secure the ends with stitches and sew the handle to the seams on the outside top edge of the bag. Make 6 tassels from the remaining ribbon (see Figs 2, 3, 4 and 5, page 81 for the technique). Sew a tassel to the handle ends and two for each side seam (see picture).

CHAPTER SIX

Developing ideas

Ideas are all around us but often, we do not look at the world sufficiently carefully to take note of what we see. When you are out and about, sketch what you see to record it and your sketch will later serve to remind you of what you saw.

Note down colour effects, weaving patterns, or patterns that might be printed or painted on ribbons, textures you might achieve by manipulating ribbons and shapes for bags, garments and household articles.

Look also at trellis patterns for ideas for spaced weaving, and tile or floor patterns for weaving ideas.

Look at fabrics for new weaves, and at nets and meshes which might be suitable grounds for weaving. It is also worth checking on new materials in needlecraft shops – sometimes, a new material may inspire you to something new in weaving. The inspiration for the black and blue fan on page 118 for instance, came to me when I saw some sequin waste. Sequin waste has holes in it, so why not weave ribbons through it? And then, what about wire mesh – or a sieve? These may seem

slightly odd ideas but an odd idea may develop into a practical idea but if you start with a practical idea the result might well be dull.

Some of my students have been combining painted or printed ribbons with some stitched ones, together with strips of embroidered fabrics, all woven together to make a wonderful rich pattern with lots of detail.

Others have worked a weaving of ribbons and strips of fabric and have then embroidered it – one of the best ideas had many tiny eyelets worked through the layers of weaving, which looked decorative and held the layers together firmly. Other weavings have been quilted, with lines and blocks of hand stitching in places. One student painted white ribbons and strips of fabric with thin bands of dark colours, and then gathered some of the fabric strips and wove them into the flat ribbons. She drew parts of this and other weavings, and has developed the drawings into a design for a wall hanging which will include some areas of ribbon weaving in it. On one occasion, my students were given as a subject for drawing a detail of a basket handle. The drawing on this page (left) is an example of one student's work. It shows a contrast of scale in the weaving, and also a three-dimensional area where the round handle is inserted into the flat side of the basket.

After this, the next stage would be for the student to work two or three samples based on the drawing, emphasizing these aspects.

The word 'design' frightens most people, but a design is only a plan. First comes the idea, and then it is must be implemented by deciding what colours and materials to use, and in what form. That is the design. ▶

Top left: A twisted weave normally used in basket making. Middle left, basket weaven pattern. Bottom left, weaving in bands over foundation cords, used by the Navajo Indians. Top right, a salish weave with verticals and diagonals enclosed in twining. Bottom right, A Japanese pattern using weaving in 5 layers

Be as receptive to your surroundings as possible and write down (and sketch) ideas as they occur. You may never refer to your notebook but, on looking back, something else may occur to you which will be used.

Experiments with weaving

Most of this book is concerned with using ribbon weaving in different ways to make items to use around the home, or wear. This chapter will endeavour to stimulate you to a more experimental approach to ribbon weaving. Some of the ideas may not seem very practical but they could be used in wall panels and hanging. Other ideas are practical for use but may take a little time to do.

When you are experimenting with a technique or with materials, some of the results may not come up to your expectations. (Equally, some might be the most beautiful and original patterns you have ever produced.) The important thing is not to be disappointed with your work but to try and try again.

The satisfaction of working out your own original thoughts is immense and you should not be deterred from trying to do something just because it has not been done before. If an experiment goes wrong it can always be unpicked and started again. But perhaps you can use the piece for another project, cut into strips and woven with other materials? Perhaps it can be applied to a piece of fabric and decorative stitches worked over the surface? Perhaps another layer of open weaving can be laid over the top? Nothing is ever entirely lost and nothing is lost by trying out an idea. The result may exceed your greatest expectations.

Other kinds of weaving

Most of the weaving patterns in this book have been worked flat, so it is worth while trying out some patterns that are not flat but have twists and loops in them. The pattern diagrams on page 109 illustrate Shii-lo weaves for baskets using round cane or other round stems. Try these weaves using a flat ribbon, letting it fold and twist as it goes over

and under. Experiment with a stuffed tubular ribbon and work several samples until you are happy with the colour combination, the texture and the proportion of the weave. You can then decide what to make with your sample, and this may necessitate changes in the pattern. You might, for instance, decide to combine stuffed and flat ribbons, or even to include another material such as fabric strips with the ribbons. It is a good idea to leave the project aside for a week or so, then come back to it and see if any new ideas occur. If you are still enthusiastic about your achievement, you are ready to begin calculating materials for the finished project.

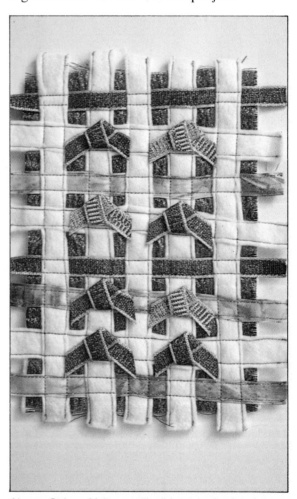

Above: Strips of felt, metallic ribbons and painted ribbons woven together with spaces so that the Lurex backing shows through. Short lengths of metallic ribbons knotted and stitched at the intersections
Right: Metallic ribbon woven through stitches and other ribbons. Folded ribbons caught with stitches and knotted narrow ribbon woven through

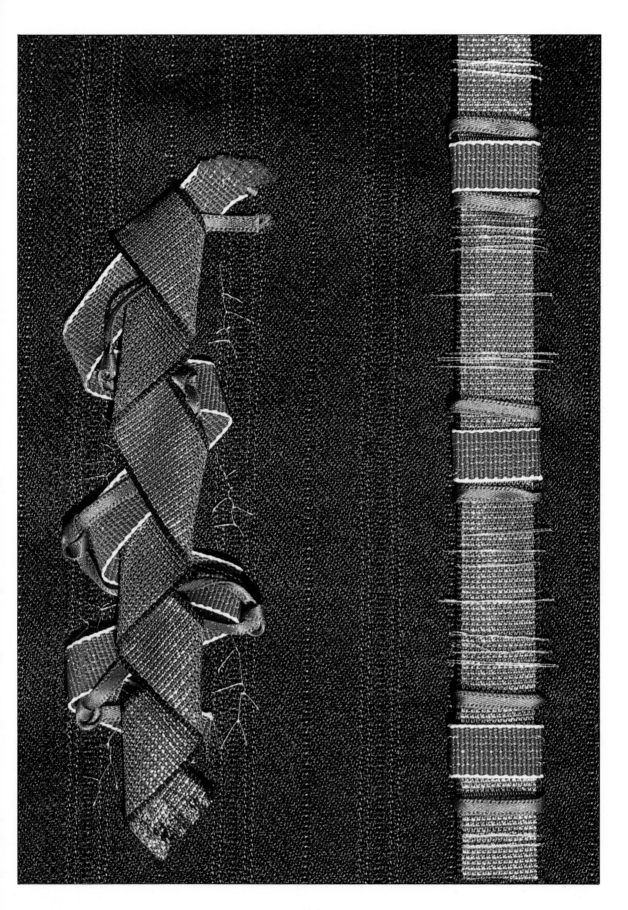

Shaggy ribbon weaving

In this technique, ribbons, strips of fabric and yarns are needlewoven into canvas and the ends knotted, so that long ends are left hanging, producing a shaggy pile.

Short ends of ribbon, mixed fabric remnants, and yarns of all kinds can be used and beautiful colour effects can be achieved.

Uses for shaggy weaving

Besides cushion covers, such as the one pictured on page 115, shaggy weaving can be used for rugs, wall hangings and panels, for bed-heads and small stool tops as well as for jackets and waistcoats and big bags and hold-alls.

Materials and equipment

Rug canvas is generally used for large projects but the technique can also be worked on finer mesh canvas to make small items. Any kinds of ribbons will do but if mixed fibres are used, the finished article can only be dry-cleaned. Strips can also be cut from the fabric remnants and tubular knitting ribbons, tapes, knitting yarns etc will all add interesting texture. Mix matt and shiny ribbons, smooth and pile textures and perhaps include transparent ribbons.

Strips and ribbons etc are cut 20 – 30cm (8 – 12 in) long and 1 – 2cm (½ – ¾ in) wide. Fabric strips can be cut wider as the fabric is crushed as it passes through the canvas holes and this adds interest to the texture.

For finer mesh canvas, very narrow ribbons, knitting and weaving yarns are used. To prevent ribbon ends ravelling and fraying, cut ends diagonally, and seal the ends of knitting ribbons by searing them on a match flame. If strips continue to fray it may be necessary to machine-stitch along the length.

A large-sized, blunt-tipped rug wool needle is used for needleweaving but check to see that the threaded needle passes through the canvas easily.

Basic technique

Cut and prepare the ribbons, strips and threads. Knot one end and thread the other end into the needle. (Very shiny, slippery knitted ribbons may need two knots.) Pass the needle through 2 or 3 threads or canvas then pull the knot onto the canvas. Slip the needle from the ribbon and tie a single over-hand knot over the needle so that you can slip the knot to lie on the canvas, leaving the ribbon end hanging. When working the weaving, choose one type of ribbon or strip and needleweave it at intervals over the canvas. Then choose the next type of strip and work this between the first. Work over the entire area in this way and gradually build up the shaggy effect, rather than starting at one edge and filling every row. In this way, the total colour effect can be judged more easily and adapted if required.

Ribbons, in particular, may tend to twist. Sometimes a twist is a good thing and adds to the effect but to prevent twists forming hold the loop of the ribbon in the left hand as you work the needleweaving and continue holding it with the thumb as the needle is pulled through.

Textures and colours

The texture of the weaving will be decided by what kind of item is being made. A cushion, such as that pictured, or a wall panel, could have a medium-length pile. A rug could be shaggier with wider fabric strips and ribbons being used. A jacket could be quite shaggy at the back with a shorter pile on the fronts.

Three ribbons of different colours can be woven in one needle. Then, for the next group, use two of the three colours plus a new colour. In the next group, use two of the three colours, plus a new colour and so on. This produces a soft, blended colour effect over the piece.

Patterns

The hanging ends of the ribbons and fabrics can be grouped to make patterns, as shown in Fig 1 and Fig 2. Draw lines on the canvas to indicate the shaggy areas, using permanent-colour felt pens in colours to match the ribbons to be used. Weave the ribbons flat until the line is reached, then leave the ends hanging. Weave very short lengths, some-times only over two or three threads of canvas within the shaggy area, then work the weaving flat again. Add extra lengths of ribbons knotted into the canvas if you wish to make it even shaggier.

You can also weave right across an article such as a bag or cushion, leaving the ends hanging at the bottom or on each side to be a finishing fringe, with the centre area left flat.

Small, repeat patterns can be worked over the surface of, perhaps, a cushion by cutting the pieces of ribbon to the same length and weaving them through the same number of canvas threads each time. For example, weave 6 lengths of ribbons through 6 threads of canvas horizontally, leaving all ends hanging. Then weave another 6 vertically next to the first block of weaving, to make a basket pattern (Fig 1). Continue to weave the ribbons in blocks, alternately horizontally and vertically, until the whole surface is covered. If the beginning of each row is staggered by dropping down one thread of canvas, a chevron pattern will result (Fig 2).

A different effect can be worked by combining two textures. Weave a fine mesh canvas with narrow ribbons and yarns, then lay it on a larger-mesh rug canvas. Weave some ribbons and yarns through both layers of canvas at the edges to hold them together. Then work the coarser areas. The edges of

the finer canvas will not show underneath the hanging ends.

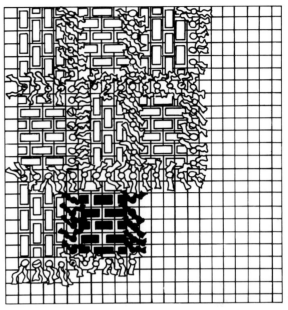

Fig 1 Shaggy weaving: short lengths of ribbons and strips of fabric woven through rug canvas, knotted at each end, ends left hanging, making a basket pattern

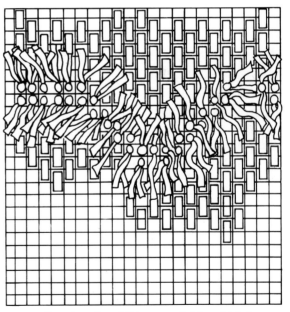

Fig 2 Short lengths of ribbons and strips of fabric woven through canvas to make a pattern, knotted at bottom edge. Further layers of knotted ribbons are added

Shaggy cushion

This cushion is made by sewing the pieces of calico together and then applying the unworked canvas to the calico cover. The weaving is done afterwards. Working in this way means that the weaving is easier to do than on a flat surface, and also the colour and texture combinations of the ribbons, tapes and yarns can be judged more easily.

Materials required
2 41cm (16¼ in)-square pieces of calico
38cm (15 in)-square cushion pad
41cm (16¼ in)-square piece of rug canvas
Cream sewing thread
Large blunt-tipped rug needle

Fabrics, ribbons and threads
An assortment of ribbons, strips of fabric, knitting ribbons and tape, raffia etc, was used to make the cushion pictured. These included white and grey 6mm (¼ in)-wide satin ribbon, white, grey and cream shiny knitting ribbon, strips of white fabric printed with small black flowers, strips of calico, strips of white suede, black knitting ribbon, stitched with white, white knitting ribbon stitched with black, Paris tape, strips of white cotton fabric and white seam binding. Approximately 4 – 5m (4⅜ – 5½ yd) each of ribbon and fabric strip was used but the quantity needed will vary according to the width of the strips. When working narrow ribbons weave two or even three thicknesses together.

Preparation
1   Draw a 36cm (14¼ in) square centrally on one piece of calico. Lay it on top of the second piece matching edges and pin them together.
2   Machine-stitch on the drawn line, leaving a 15cm (6 in) opening in the middle of one side for turning. Trim the corners diagonally.
3   Turn right side out. Press and pin the open edges together.
4   Turn the edges of the rug canvas under to make a 35.5cm (14 in) square, matching holes in the top and lower layers at the edges.
5   Pin the calico cushion cover to the wrong side of the rug canvas, covering the turned edges, matching corners and edges. Pin at right angles on the edges.
6   Begin stitching 2cm (¾ in) from a corner, then work on 3 sides and 2cm (¾ in) of the fourth side. Stitch just inside the cushion cover seam line and stitch twice for strength.
7   Insert the cushion pad, pushing the corners well down into the cover.
8   Pin and then oversew the open seam using doubled thread.
9   Cut the various ribbons, fabrics, tapes, yarns etc into 30cm (12 in) pieces, cutting ends diagonally, or sealing ends.

Weaving
10   Tie a knot in the ribbon end or fabric strip and thread the other end into the needle. Needleweave through 4 or 5 canvas threads, pulling the knot up so that it lies on the canvas. Slip the needle from the strip and allow the end to hang. Tie a knot in the strip, sliding the knot to lie on the canvas. The knots will secure the strip.
11   Stagger the beginnings and endings and fill up any thin areas with extra lengths of narrow ribbons.

Work yarns and tapes in the same way, inserting them into the canvas at random (see picture).
12   Trim all the ribbons, yarns and tape ends to about 8cm (3¼ in).

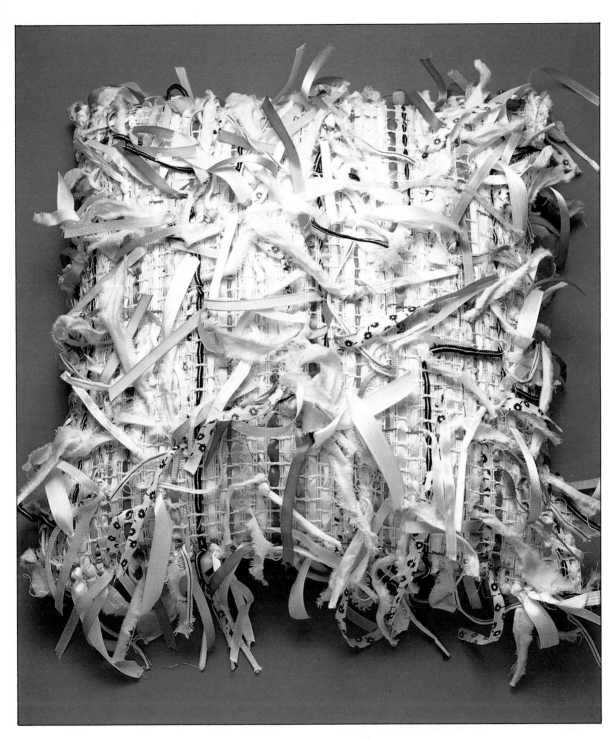

The shaggy cushion technique can also be used to make large floor cushions for children's play rooms. The shaggy pile is hardwearing and the knots will stand up to any amount of rough treatment.

Cut calico into two 1m (1⅛ yd) squares. Cut rug canvas to the same size and turn the edges under. Make up the calico cushion cover (as for the small cushion already described) and stitch the rug canvas to the calico cover. As this is a large area of canvas to cover, it might be a good idea to use more fabric strips, using ribbon for colour and textural interest. When the weaving is completed, cut the ends of the strips and ribbons to 8cm (3¼ in) long.

Three-dimensional effects in ribbon weaving

There are various ways of weaving ribbons to achieve a three-dimensional shape, or a raised surface. A tubular ribbon stuffed will produce a thick, firm fabric when woven and can also be twisted or looped to add to the effect. Balls or knobs can be woven with either flat or stuffed ribbons using the methods usually used with string or rope. Buttons, balls for the end of cords, and balls which can be used as blind pulls or light switches can all be made.

Weaving with knots and loops

Knots, twists and loops in ribbon gives weaving a superb texture, especially if the work is done with a stiff ribbon. Modern polyester ribbons have considerable 'bounce', unlike the softer acetate, rayon or silk ribbons which do not knot so well. Fig 1 shows a twist which is sometimes used when making baskets, and which would be effective worked in ribbons machine-stitched with different coloured threads on the top of the machine and the bobbin.

When making knots in ribbons, keep the knot in the correct place by slipping a large needle into the loop of the knot and then sliding the loop along the ribbon to the desired position.

Twisted and looped ribbons can be woven into many of the weaving patterns on pages 20–21, 22–23. The warp can be worked flat, and the weft ribbons then twisted, looped or knotted. Alternatively, the warp ribbons can be twisted and the weft knotted as it is woven through it. It is also possible to move up and down from one row to another, twisting the ribbon as you go.

Instead of weaving from one end of a row to the other, try weaving for a short length, and changing direction to come back to the beginning again. Make a loop or twist where you changed direction. Start another ribbon and weave to fill in different spaces over the warp, again twisting and looping at every change of direction. Gradually the whole area will be woven, but as you can change colours or types of ribbon for every area, you will have blocks of colour instead of lines. All the beginnings and endings can be hidden at the back of the work.

Very narrow ribbons can be looped over wide ones, or wide ribbons over narrow ones. The wide ribbons will crush where they are knotted or twisted, so giving a different texture. Transparent ribbons can be mixed with velvet ones, and printed or striped ribbons with plain.

The spacing is important too, and the ribbons can be closely woven, or spaces left between them.

Ribbon can also be knotted, twisted or looped when woven through fabrics. Separate knots or bows could be applied to the surface of the weaving to give additional texture.

Round weave

This is a classic woven shape and follows a regular over and under sequence. Follow the

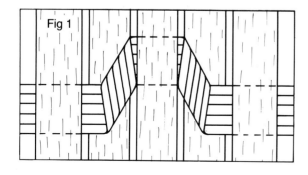

diagrams Fig 1 to Fig 4 (right). Check the intersections of the weave very carefully to avoid mistakes. If preferred, the weave can be worked on a cork mat, pinning the loops in place. From Fig 3, continue weaving by running the end of the ribbon parallel to the previous rows, until the desired number is reached. Weaving should be firm so that it keeps its shape. Finish the ends by sewing them under a previous row.

On a small scale, these knots are used as frogs and applied to clothes as fastenings. On a larger scale, they can become mats.

Monkey's fist

These woven knots can be used on the ends of cords. They make good buttons for bags and clothes, or can be sewn to a purchased ear-ring fitting.

1 Start as shown in Fig 1 (below) by making three circuits round the hand from left to right.
2 The ribbon then goes horizontally round from the right hand side, round the back to the left, and returning to the right hand side (Fig 2).
3 Repeat two more horizontal circuits, each moving about the other (Fig 3).
4 Remove from your hand and make three more vertical circuits around the previous set (Fig 4).
5 Tighten up the slack to make a firm ball.

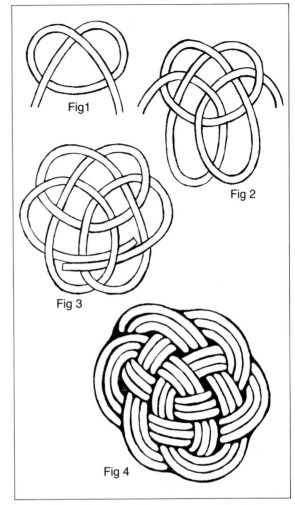

Above: To work the round weave, weave the ribbon as shown in Fig 1 to Fig 4 until the desired size is obtained. Finish ends by sewing them underneath

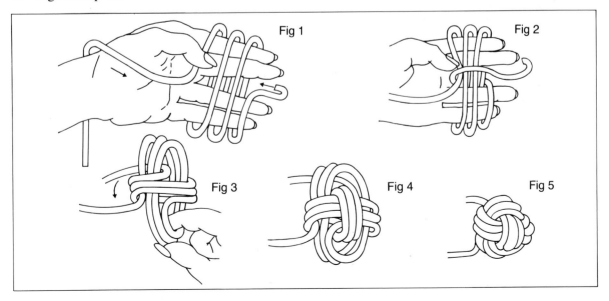

117

Weaving through sequin waste

When you first begin working a sample based on a fresh idea or when you are trying out a new material or method, you tend to work in a straightforward way. Then, while you are working, another idea comes to you and you begin another sample. While you are working on the second sample, another idea comes into your head and you wonder why you have not thought of that before.

You might then begin to plan what you can do with this new idea and perhaps decide on a specific item that you want to make.

Then the method you have chosen proves not to be entirely satisfactory, so a third trial begins.

If all goes well after this, you might be ready to start on your new project.

The bonus of doing all these trials and experiments is that one of the stages will probably prove to be right for something else entirely, so that you have two projects to work on instead of just one.

Nothing is ever completely wasted and everything you try is part of the learning process.

Weaving through sequin waste started without my having any end product in mind. The experiments were originally to find out which ribbons looked well with sequin waste, whether they should be solid or transparent, which colours looked best and whether the weaving should be flat or have loops or twists in it.

It seemed to me that machine-embroidery could be worked on top of the sequin waste and the logical step from that seemed to be to stitch on the sequin waste before the ribbons were woven through. Close zigzag machine-stitching was therefore worked down each line of the waste in one direction

Sequin waste fan

I wanted to use the method on a fan and the only way it seemed possible was to cut short lengths of sequin waste, weave short lengths of narrow ribbons through them and then trap the cut lengths between net. More stitchery had to be worked on top to secure it all. The result can be seen on page 119.

Preparation

1   Bend a piece of wire to the fan's shape.
2   Frame a piece of net in a large embroidery ring.
3   Lay the wire shape on the net.
4   Set the machine at width 4 and stitch over the wire 2 all round or 3 times.

Weaving

5   Cut sequin waste into strips 5 – 7cm (2 – 2¾ in) long and weave 1.5 mm (¹⁄₁₆ in)-wide ribbons through each strip.
   Leave the ribbons long at each end.
6   Lay the strips on the net at different angles and machine-stitch across the fan to secure them. The stitching should go over the wire frame at the beginning of each journey.
7   Remove the work from the frame, lay another piece of net on top and pin the net layers together round the outside of the wire.
8   Work more machine-stitching across the net and over the frame.
9   Paint the whole fan with PVA glue, which will dry transparent.
10   Add more decoration in the way of bows of ribbons, beads and feathers etc.
11   Knot narrow ribbon over the wire frame all round to make a fringe.
12   Push the two ends of the frame into a piece of bamboo or a perspex rod, and wrap the rod with ribbon to cover it.

Two fans

Fixed fans, or handscreens as they were sometimes called, are common in Europe as well as in China, Japan and India. Fans have been made from paper, wood, cane, split bamboo, pierced leather, jade, silk, plaited straw, ivory, and embroidered fabrics – so why not from woven ribbons?

The shape of the white fan (pictured on page 119) is based on an Indian design and is made from plastic canvas woven with a variety of ribbons. Wire mesh or cotton canvas (which could be painted or stitched before the ribbons are threaded through) could also be used. The blue and black fan (page 119) is made on the wire frame of a Chinese paper fan.

White fan

Materials
19 × 24cm (7½ × 9½ in) piece plastic canvas, 3 holes to 1cm (³⁄₈ in)
2 114cm (45 in)-long plastic or acrylic rods, wooden dowels or bamboo sticks
2m (2¼ yd) lengths of wider ribbon or knitting ribbon
6m (6⁵⁄₈ yd) of 1.5mm (¹⁄₁₆ in)-wide ribbon
An assortment of other narrow ribbons and knitting ribbons, including 2 lengths of 2m (2¼ yd) each

Preparation
1   Make a pattern from the diagram Fig 1. Use the pattern to cut the shape from canvas with the threads running vertically and horizontally.
2   Lay one rod on each side of the canvas along the centre line (see pattern) and secure temporarily.
3   Cut 2m (2¼ yd) of the 1.5mm (¹⁄₁₆ in) ribbon and thread it into a blunt-tipped needle. Sew, very tightly, over and over both rods to hold them in place.
4   Using the 2m (2¼ yd) lengths of ribbon or knitting ribbon, and starting at one side, weave it up and down the fan through the canvas. Hold the starting end at the back of the canvas and then weave over it. Leave the finishing end of the ribbon end hanging at the top end of the fan. Leave at least 12cm (4¾ in) hanging.
5   Work the other side of the fan in the same way.
6   With the remaining lengths of ribbon, weave through the main part of the canvas, leaving the ends hanging at the top. Make sure that ribbons of different textures are used on the centre panel of the fan or it will look too flat. If you prefer not to have the ribbon ends hanging, hold them at the back of the fan when it is in use. Alternatively, weave the ends in. To cover the fan, 5 or 6 lengths will be needed. As new lengths are introduced lay them over the end of the one preceding.

Blue and black fan

Materials
Chinese paper fan with a wire frame
Wooden ring embroidery frame 26cm (10¼ in) diameter
45cm (18 in) of black dress net with hexagonal mesh
10cm (4 in) pieces of black, royal blue and turquoise sequin waste
Black machine-embroidery thread
1.10m (1¼ yd) of 3mm (¹⁄₈ in)-wide black satin ribbon
2.15m (2³⁄₈ yd) of 1.5mm (¹⁄₁₆ in)-wide royal blue satin ribbon

120

2.15m (2³⁄₈ yd) of 1.5mm (¹⁄₁₆ in)-wide turquoise satin ribbon
2.15m (2³⁄₈ yd) of 1.5mm (¹⁄₁₆ in)-wide black satin ribbon
2m (2¹⁄₄ yd) of 1.5mm (¹⁄₁₆ in)-wide navy satin ribbon

Preparation

1 Tear the paper away from the fan exposing the wire frame.

2 Using the black machine-embroidery thread, work zigzag satin-stitch over the frame to cover it.

3 Mount 1 layer of the net in the embroidery frame. Lay the fan in the centre

Fig 1   Draw a pattern for the white fan from the measurements given

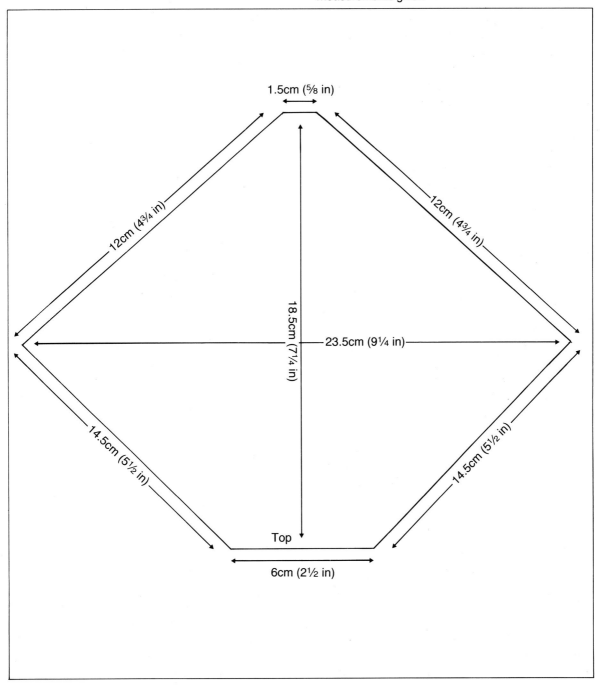

of the net, with the handle over the edge. Zigzag-stitch over the wire frame to attach the net. Remove the net and fan from the embroidery frame.

4   Cut short lengths of sequin waste, 1 row of holes wide. Cut the narrow ribbons slightly longer than the sequin waste, and weave them through the strips.

5   Arrange the strips of woven sequin waste on the fan, lying in different directions. Lay a second piece of net on top and pin round the outside of the wire frame, and on the inside of the frame.

6   Machine-stitch across the fan from side to side through the woven ribbons, over the edge and back again. A lot of stitching should be worked as this strengthens the fan.

7   Trim the excess net away from the outside edges.

8   Using the 3mm (⅛ in)-wide black ribbon, wrap the handle to cover it, starting at the bottom. Finish the end by knotting it through the wire frame at the top of the handle.

9   Cut 20cm (8 in) lengths of the narrow ribbons and knot them round the edges of the fan to make the fringe.

Decoration can be added in the form of small ribbon bows, beads, or feathers sewn on by hand using matching thread.

Making fan frames

To make a delicate looking fan frame bend a strong piece of wire round a large can to make a circular fan, or a wooden box, to make a square or rectangular fan. Leave 10 – 15cm (4 – 6 in) ends for the handle and twist them together. Push the ends into a piece of bamboo or acrylic rod securing them in place with a strong contact adhesive dripped into the rod first.

Other structures can be used to make fans, hexagonal or pentagonal shapes made from wood dowelling or acrylic rods and wrapped to hold them where they cross.

Right: Sequin waste covered with machine-couched metallic threads and narrow ribbons woven through leaving loops at intervals   *Barbara Furze*

Below: Strips of space-dyed fabric woven through sequin waste with machine-stitching threads crossing and 'blobs' of stitches securing the layers

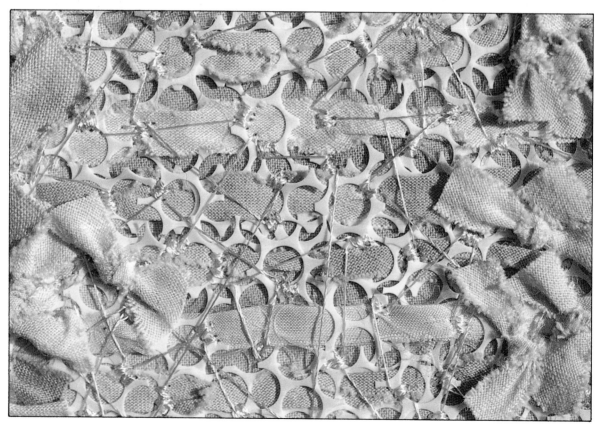

Not the end

Now that this book is finished, I find I have so many more ideas on how to weave with ribbons, and what to make with the weaving. In fact, a second book would be possible. When I first tried ribbon weaving it seemed a slightly limited field; now it seems that years would not be too long to spend on the subject, and that the techniques in this book could be adapted to make almost anything in the world.

There are still some areas not even tried: for instance, ribbon weaving could be laminated or painted with resin to make it stiff and waterproof and this opens up possibilities for making table mats, umbrellas, bowls and dishes, and covers for garden chairs. It might be possible to paint the weaving with two or three coats of PVA glue which dries totally transparent.

Another area that has not been investigated fully is weaving with ribbons on a loom. I am not a weaver so using a loom does not come naturally to me, but it might to one of my readers.

Whatever your particular skill, it can probably be adapted to working with ribbons, and you may come up with something quite new and exciting.

The projects in this book are starting points only, and once one or two patterns have been tried (and varied according to your own ideas) I hope you will develop and experiment with other methods, and perhaps produce other, different, methods and designs. Ribbons are luxurious and it is worth taking time and trouble to make beautiful things with them. The results will certainly be appreciated by your family and friends, and you will feel great satisfaction in a project well done.

Valerie Campbell-Harding

Bibliography

Embroidered boxes and other construction techniques Jane Lemon (Batsford). For advice on making boxes, bags, lampshades, cushions and book covers.

Beginner's guide to fabric dyeing and printing Stuart and Patricia Robinson (Newnes). Ideas on printing and dyeing.

Church embroidery Beryl Dean (Mowbray). Making up church articles.

The structure of weaving Ann Sutton (Batsford). Weaving patterns and ideas for texture.

Simple Weaving Hilary Chetwynd (Studio Vista). Weaving patterns.

Textile techniques in Metal Arline M. Fisch (Van Nostrand Reinhold). Ideas for flat and three-dimensional weaving.

Rugs from Rags John Hinchcliffe and Angela Jeffs. A section on weaving through knitting.

Fashion with ribbon Kay Anderson (Batsford). Ideas for ribbon weaving on clothes.

The technique of filet lace Pauline Knight (Batsford). Netting instructions and patterns.

Useful addresses

Old ribbons
Fumbles (period clothes), 66 High Street,
Great Missenden, Buckinghamshire

Indian woven ribbons
Oriental department, Liberty, Regent Street,
London W1
Iqbal Sari & Textile House, 394-396
Stapleton Road, Bristol, Avon

**Vilene pelmet-weight, iron-on and bonding
interfacings**
Information from Vilene Organisation, PO
Box 3, Greetland, Halifax HX4 8NJ

Satin bias binding
Crown Needlework, High Street,
Hungerford, Berkshire

Knit-weave needles
Smallwares Ltd, 17 Galena Road, King
Street, Hammersmith, London W6 0LN

Embroidery threads
Mace & Nairn, 89 Crane Street, Salisbury,
Wiltshire

Rubber printing stamps
Philip & Tacey, North Way, Andover,
Hampshire

Japanese flower ribbons
Hamilworth Floral Products, 23 Lime Road,
Dumbarton, Dumbartonshire

Net and mesh fabrics
Borovicks, 16 Berwick Street, London W1V
4HP
Shades, 57 Candlemass Lane, Beaconsfield,
Buckinghamshire (suppliers of French
square mesh net)
J.M. Russell, 622 Bristol Road South,
Northfield, Birmingham B31 2JR

Fabric paints
Shades, 57 Candlemass Lane, Beaconsfield,
Buckinghamshire
Terry Taylor Associates, 27 Woodland
Road, Tunbridge Wells, Kent TN4 9HW
George Weil, 63-65 Riding House Street,
London W1P 7PP

Knitting ribbons
Ries Wools, 242-243 High Holborn, London
WC1V 7 DZ
Creativity, 45 New Oxford Street, London
WC1 and Downing Street, Farnham,
Surrey
Knitters of Dent, Main Street, Dent,
Sedburgh, Cumbria LA10 5OL

Index